MW00880696

# MEMOIRS

## OF A

# MASTER

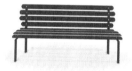

*Adamus Saint-Germain*

*through*
*Geoffrey and Linda Hoppe*

# Memoirs of a Master

**CRIMSON CIRCLE**

Published by Crimson Circle Press,
a division of the Crimson Circle Energy Company, Inc.
PO Box 7394
Golden, Colorado USA
Contact: customerservice@crimsoncircle.com
Web: www.crimsoncircle.com

ISBN 978-1540320469

First Printing, November 2016

Printed in the United States of America

Cover Design: Geoffrey Hoppe
Book Design and Layout: Geoffrey Hoppe and Jean Tinder
Transcription: Gail Neube
Editing and Proofing: Jean Tinder and Maija Leisso

*This book is dedicated to the
Master and the student within each of us.*

*The Master is the wise and patient inner voice, always
present, always compassionate, but oftentimes unheard
by the student with all of the noise from everyday human
life. The Master is already within, already Realized,
already enlightened, and never more than a breath away.*

*The student is the eager learner, the doubtful human,
the terrified yet determined seeker. The student knows
there is more to life, but doesn't know what it is or how
to get there. In spite of this, the student continues on
the path, driven by an unrelenting quest to unite with
their deep inner knowingness, no matter how long it
takes or what sacrifices must be endured.*

*In this book, as in life,
the Master and the human are but the same.*

# MEMOIRS of a MASTER

# Contents

# Welcome

This is a book of short stories told by Adamus Saint-Germain as part of his lectures to audiences around the world. The stories are based on or inspired by actual experiences of the many people who have been guided and taught by Adamus.

These stories are designed to help you see yourself as both the Master and the student. There's no secret coding in the words, no deep esoteric meaning beyond the simple narratives. The student is generally a compilation of many people rather than just one person, and the stories take place in contemporary life rather than in the past or future. The Master can be either female, male or both, depending on your personal preference. The Master can be perceived as Adamus or any other enlightened teacher, but ultimately it's you.

The stories are based on some of the more complex teachings of Adamus Saint-Germain. By putting some of this sacred information into story form, it becomes more personal, more understandable and perhaps more entertaining. But within each story are profound insights as well as many layers of wisdom.

Don't try to read too much (or too little) into these stories. Take them for what they are, and feel the energy contained within the words. And, at any time while you're reading them, feel free to call on Adamus to share your own experiences into embodied enlightenment.

# Story 1

# The Loan

*Inspired by one man's real issues...*

The Master was fishing at a beautiful lake on a warm sunny afternoon. He loved fishing, because it gave him a chance to be in nature and also to practice his natural abilities of abundance. The moment he threw the line in the water, a fish would bite, even though there wasn't any bait on the hook. Then he would reel the fish in, admire its beauty, and of course throw it back into the lake. It was almost effortless. For the Master, this was an excellent way of experiencing the simple spiritual truth that *all things come to you... if you Allow.*

The Master was enjoying the solitude of this lovely day at the lake, when suddenly he heard rustling in the bushes behind him. He turned around to see Richard, one of his students, approaching him with a look of exasperation.

The Master took a deep breath and muttered to himself, "Here we go again."

Richard looked and sounded exasperated. "Master! There you are! I need your help. Everything is going wrong. In spite of all the classes I've taken, in spite of all the studying I've done, I am in worse condition than ever.

"I'm broke and unable to pay my bills. My car is in the shop and I don't have enough money to get it out. I'm behind on my mortgage payments and there's a good chance that I'm going to lose my house. I barely have enough food to eat. Master, what can I do? Tell me something, anything. I'm right on the edge. I'm not even sure I want to live anymore!"

The Master chuckled quietly to himself, because he had heard this story so many times before, from Richard and others like him. It was, indeed, a moment of desperation, but it was also potentially important because moments like these are when humans are able to make the greatest changes in their lives. Or not.

The Master said, "Dear Richard, how much money do you need to solve your problems?" Richard looked a little surprised at the Master's willingness – he had expected a long lecture from the Master about abundance – and quickly said, "Master, I only need five thousand dollars."

A voice balloon appeared above the Master's head, but Richard couldn't see it: "Stupid Richard, he should have asked for fifty thousand dollars. But he's so desperate, and so limited in his thoughts and imagination, that he asked only for five thousand dollars." The Master paused for a long time, intentionally playing out the whole drama with Richard and actually rather enjoying it, because, in Richard, the Master saw himself from about five lifetimes ago. Back then he was still desperate, still feeding off of other people's energy, and, in spite of all the classes, schools and teachings, still insisting that his life was created by things outside of himself, rather than within himself.

At last the Master said "Richard, I'll loan you the money." The Master reached into his pocket and, even though he hadn't put any money in his wallet earlier that day, he suddenly found five thousand dollars, exactly what was needed. The Master didn't even remember where he got the money. It was just there, and he didn't question it. That's the way it is with Masters.

As the Master counted out the money, one hundred dollars at time, Richard's eyes grew wide. He could hardly believe the Master was actually giving him this money. Now he could pay his bills, fix his car and solve many of his problems. Richard promised a lot of things in this moment of desperation. "I'll pay you back, Master, with interest!" The Master laughed to himself, "There goes Richard, lying again."

Richard continued, "Master, I'll never ever forget what you've done for me." The Master laughed again and said, "Actually, one of these days you'll either forget me or betray me, but it doesn't matter."

As soon as the Master finished counting out the money, Richard quickly ran off. The Master went back to fishing, pulling in one fish after the other. "So easy it is," he thought. "Fishing is like life. It just comes to you. You take what you need and you put the rest back, but you never limit yourself."

\* \* \*

Six months later, the Master was sitting at an outdoor café, once again enjoying the beautiful weather and having a triple-shot caramel macchiato with three chocolate croissants. The Master didn't diet, and he never worried about calories, carbs, sugar, gluten or fat. He could eat anything – whether it came from the sky, the land or the ocean – and it didn't matter. It didn't matter if his food was gluten-free or free-range, whether it was organic or processed, kosher or forbidden. His body always responded appropriately to remain in balance. The Master was in command of his body and his energy; therefore, he could eat or drink anything he chose.

While sipping his macchiato at the café, he happened to look up and see Richard trudging by. His clothes were tattered, his hair was disheveled, his beard unkempt, his sandals worn out. From head to toe, Richard looked a mess.

The Master called out, "Richard! Come here for a moment. Sit down and have a cup of coffee with me." Richard stammered, "But I … I don't have any money." The Master said with false sympathy, "Well, that's too bad. I guess you can watch me enjoy mine!"

Now, only six months had passed since the Master had lent Richard five thousand dollars. You would think he could at least buy Richard a cup of plain coffee now. But the Master was tired of playing the game. He said, "Richard, what happened? What happened to the money? What happened to your life?"

"Master, it was terrible! After you gave me the money, I paid some of my bills and got my car out of the shop, but a week later I was in a terrible accident that totaled the car. Then I lent some money to a friend who never paid it back. On top of that, I was robbed one night while walking home and lost every last dollar."

Richard continued, "Master, I'm more in debt than I ever was. Please, I promise to never, ever ask you again, but would it be possible to loan me another five thousand dollars? I'll be able to repay all of the money in no more than six months, with interest, of course."

The Master took a deep breath and said, "No Richard. I wanted to prove a point to you, and I did. The point is this: you're in a pattern, and you're not willing to get out of it. It's a habitual pattern – a consciousness of 'just enough' – and whether I had given you ten thousand dollars or fifty thousand dollars, you'd still manage to lose everything. Six months ago, I could have told you that we'd meet like this, that you would once again be broke and desperate, and once again lying to yourself. Once was enough, Richard. No more. As a matter of fact, not only do you owe me the five thousand dollars plus interest, you also owe for all the classes you've never paid for. I don't want to see you again until you have fully repaid every last dollar."

\* \* \*

Many people are living Richard's story. It's the story of being stuck in victim consciousness and living it out accordingly. If you give a victim a million dollars, two years later he'll be in debt two million dollars. It's a pattern. It's energy feeding. It's lack of responsibility. *It's an abundance of non-abundance.* People like poor Richard tend to stay in the same consciousness, even if they're shown a way out. They'll make every sort of excuse to justify their situation, but rarely will they make a conscious choice to change. Why? Because they're still getting something from playing the victim role.

Abundance is a God-gifted, natural condition. From the moment Spirit blessed you with the breath of life, you've had all the abundance and energy you'll ever need. Yet so many people get caught up in playing the victim game, making excuses, blaming others and insisting on their life of lack. They muddle in the consciousness of *Just Barely Enough* rather than allowing natural abundance to flow into their lives.

There is *no one other than you* that's holding you back. It doesn't matter where you live or what jobs you've had. It doesn't matter whether you come from a rich family or a poor family, whether you're smart or stupid, male or female. None of those things matter. The moment you consciously choose abundance, it will start serving you.

The only thing that matters is whether you're ready to allow abundance into your life in a joyful, fulfilling, wealthy and gifted way; or whether you are going to continue down the path of *Just Barely Enough*.

Like Richard, many have battled and struggled with abundance. They've tried all sorts of gimmicks to bring abundance into their life, but they just don't work, especially when they're stuck in patterns like Richard. He received a significant loan from the Master, and then literally directed that money right back into his old patterns.

Are you *really* ready for true abundance? If you are, it will be there, just like the fish coming to the Master. It's that easy. There are no gimmicks, no programs, no secrets, and no magic formulas. It's about realizing that energy is everywhere, without limit. It's about realizing that you're *already* abundant, even if it's an abundance of *Just Barely Enough*.

# Story 2

# Twenty-One Days

*Inspired by Kuthumi lal Singh*

Patrick lay in his bed, finally beginning to feel a glimmer of hope. He had just been through one of the worst periods of his entire life, enduring twenty-one days of unrelenting physical illness, mental chaos, confusion and hopelessness, hardly knowing where he was or what was happening. During these twenty-one days he had been totally alone, barely even able to feed himself due to being in such a state of chaos and illness.

It started out with his physical body feeling ill. He thought it was a cold or flu, but none of the symptoms seemed to make any sense. He didn't want to go to a doctor, because he knew from previous experience that very few in the healthcare industry really understood what happens with someone who is going through their awakening and into enlightenment. So he languished in bed for twenty-one days, never sure whether he was dreaming or awake, what was real and what wasn't.

It was a horrific experience. Patrick had to face himself in the darkest and worst ways that he could possibly imagine at the same time that his body was experiencing great pain, profuse sweating, and often feeling so cold that no amount of heat or blankets could relieve his physical suffering. It was the worst agony he could remember, and there were times when he wished he would just die and be released from the physical body.

Sometimes he cursed himself for ever thinking about awakening or pursuing any spiritual interest whatsoever, for now in his great physical and mental agony, none of the words from any teachers could possibly fix his miserable situation, let alone make any sense.

Finally, after twenty-one days of absolute misery, he started to come out of this wretched awful darkness, still unsure of who he was or what had happened. He was still filled with doubt, uncertainty and a lot of conflict, but he could feel that something had shifted in these three weeks. Something had changed.

Suddenly, he noticed the Master standing beside his bed. Patrick thought to himself, "I really don't like this, the Master just suddenly appearing. I didn't hear footsteps. He didn't knock at the door or announce himself, and in my current state, I don't even know if he's actually here or not." But another part of him was relieved to see the Master. It meant he was returning to some degree of coherence; to something he could identify with. The fact that the Master was there meant he had either come through this very difficult period or he was dead. Either one would be a relief.

Finally, Patrick spoke. "Dear Master, it felt like I died. Am I dead?" The Master looked down at Patrick, lying there on the bed. He felt a twinge of sadness as he remembered his own very difficult experience of being totally ripped apart in every way, feeling lost, confused and like he had truly been in hell.

The Master said, "No, my friend, you're not dead. You are very much alive. In fact, Patrick, you could say that before this experience is when you were actually dead. You were living in such great limitation and fear, not realizing the true I Am, and to me that is more dead than simply letting go of the physical body. But, dear Patrick, you have come through this and you are very much alive."

The student breathed a deep sigh of relief. He had endured these very difficult twenty-one days and survived. Then he asked, "Master, will this be the last time I ever have to experience this punishing, unrelenting chaos in my body and mind?"

The Master took a deep breath and said, "No, Patrick, it's not the last time. Even an Ascended Master will still go through intense periods of cleansing and releasing. When you are associated with the things and people of Earth, and with your own self as a human, you're going to accumulate the dirt and imbalances of the vibrational dualistic state.

"Living in the human condition here on Earth is unnatural. It's an amazing experience, but it's not natural. And when you embody yourself in it, you'll pick up the imbalances, the dirt and the grime of life. So you will indeed go through this again, but from now on you'll go through it as the observer. You won't be so intimately involved and caught up in it, and you won't question whether you're going to survive, because you'll already know you will. Yes, the body might get sick and the mind might get confused. But as the observer, as the Master, you'll realize you've already come through it. Now it's just about allowing that very natural process of cleansing and renewing to take place."

Patrick asked, "But can't I do this cleansing in some other realm or dimension? Going through it here on Earth is so terribly difficult."

"No," the Master answered, "Because you're accumulating it here. You're going through the experiences here in this dimension, so you have to cleanse yourself here. You have to do it from within, right where you are.

"Remember, dear Patrick, as you go through these experiences in the future, you'll be the observer. In these last twenty-one days, you weren't the observer. You were, in a way, the victim. You were so deep into the experience that you couldn't see how you had already come through it. You were so caught up in the pain, doubt and fear that you couldn't see it was simply a time of rejuvenation and cleansing. Your doubts clouded your true knowingness to the point that you forgot who you were. You forgot your own I Am, Patrick, and *that* will not happen again."

Patrick took another deep breath, relieved to know he would never have to go through that level of doubt and anguish again. Then he said, "So, what will I be now that I've gone through this deepest, most unforgiving and relentless transformation? Who am I now?"

The Master thought for a moment, remembering when he asked this very same question to his Master. Now that the old identity has been totally pulverized, now that one has been totally disconnected from the old self, what happens next? He smiled, took a deep breath and said, "Patrick, you tried so hard to hold onto your old identity. In spite of saying that you were on the spiritual path and choosing enlightenment, every time enlightenment tried to come to you, every time true Realization stood right in front of you, you kept holding onto your old identity. Even though the old identity was not asleep or unawakened, it was still highly limited. You were trying to enlighten the old identity of Patrick, rather than allowing *all* of you, all of the I Am, to be the enlightened one.

"You tried to call it enlightenment, even though you were really just trying to make life a little easier and a little better for Patrick. You were living within the greatest duality that a human can ever know – the duality of saying on one hand that you wanted freedom and enlightenment, while, on the other hand, doing everything you could to hang on to your limitations, your old identity, your singularity, your old self.

"Is it any wonder, Patrick, that these past few years of your life have been torturous in so many ways? Is it any wonder that you felt you were being false to yourself in so many ways? Is it any wonder that you were constantly out of sync with yourself and the rest of the world these past few years? Is it any wonder that your energy levels were low? Your energy was going to the effort of trying to protect your old identity from the outside world, from yourself, and even from enlightenment. You became exhausted and confused because your energy was going to all the shields and walls you placed around you, all the games and pretending.

"For so many years now, you've lived in a state of great inner conflict, waging a great battle with yourself. You've been trying so hard to be spiritual and do the right thing, while at the same time, whether you realized it or not, trying to simply embellish your old identity. And it doesn't work. That's why you ended up with these twenty-one days of intense, unrelenting, brutalizing compassion.

"From here on, there is no more Patrick, unless you want there to be. You're not singular anymore. You're no longer limited to one expression or identity. Now, as they say in the ancient language, you are *mu*. You are nothing. You do not exist anymore. You've been crushed and torn out of existence, nothing left. From this moment on, you are nothingness.

"But nothingness is like silence. It is full, for even in silence it's not quiet. Nothingness is anything you want to be. You are no longer attached to just trying to be a better Patrick or just making a better life for yourself. And you will certainly never again be attached to what you call enlightenment or spirituality, for that was really just a game for Patrick to build up and embellish his old identity.

"The beauty and grandness of it is that you *did* get enlightenment. Ultimately, after all the brutalizing and demolishing of the old singularity, you did get it. You became everything in the nothingness. You no longer have to focus on Patrick. You are no longer singular. You are no longer just living or just dead, masculine or feminine. You become all things.

"The beauty of this nothingness is that it frees you to the true act of consciousness. In other words, dear former Patrick, any consciousness that you choose henceforth, you can act out. You see, in the very limited state of Patrick, it wasn't an act; it was the only reality. You didn't view yourself as acting. You viewed yourself as just living. But when you finally allow your Realization, it's like freeing your consciousness. Then you can act and be anything you want. You can be a magi or a simpleton. You can be both together at the same time. You can be an embodied Master or one who is totally unaware of anything beyond their field of vision. You can be both at the same time. You can be abundant and non-abundant at the same time.

"The beauty is that you have freed yourself to act in any way you want, and to be conscious of it. The old Patrick wasn't really conscious. You were so singular that you were unaware of anything other than the survival of Patrick. Now that you are free, you can act and be anything you choose. It is truly the act of consciousness, expressed however you wish. That, dear Patrick, is freedom.

"Imagine not being locked into a single definition of yourself. Imagine no longer being in this great conflict with yourself, but rather free to act, to apply consciousness to anything."

Patrick took a deep breath and said, "So, am I enlightened now, dear Master?"

The Master smiled and said, "If you choose to be."

∗   ∗   ∗

Dear reader, whether you take it literally or figuratively, this is *your* story. You have been going through a great internal battle, telling yourself you're doing all this work for your enlightenment, but essentially trying to enlighten your Patrick, your singularity, your human identity. The beautiful thing about enlightenment is that it is natural. It cannot be controlled, even by your Patrick, your human self; it cannot be manipulated by that singular 'trying to make life a little better' human personality.

Your enlightenment isn't there because you asked for it or begged for it or because you're really sincere about it. It is there because it's who you really are. Your enlightenment isn't something that you can manipulate or manage. You can pretend to for a while, but true enlightenment is unrelenting. It is brutal in its compassion. It will release you from your limitations and give you your freedom, no matter what it takes; no matter how many tormented nights; no matter how many diseases; no matter how many illnesses, bad relationships or anything else. Your enlightenment, your Realization is there in full compassion, but it isn't just for the limited human holding this book.

The fact is that the Realization back into your true nature, your true I Am-ness that's so far beyond Patrick, is going to happen anyway. It's going to happen sooner or later to every human on Earth.

So what to do with your Patrick?

Take a deep breath and relax into the experience. Allow. Realize that even the hardest days and darkest nights, even this torturous inner duality is there for a reason. It's not for a lesson or to prove anything. It's there in the greatest compassion of enlightenment. There is really nothing new. It is about Allowing. I know that may seem too simple, too easy. But, dear friend, that's the way it is.

You might go through your own version of Patrick's experience of feeling just awful, like you're being torn apart, wondering if you're going to survive. In fact, I assure you right now that you *will* go through this. When it happens, simply take a deep breath and be the observer. Don't try to pretend it's not happening. Don't try to whitewash it and cover it up. Don't try to process it and figure it out. It's there for a reason. Stop wondering if you're doing it wrong. You're not. You can't. It's a cleansing and a releasing that's coming over you, and it's helping you realize that it's not your Patrick who's becoming enlightened. It's You, *all* of you.

# Story 3

# The Land of Blue

*Based on many human stories...*

Nearly every evening the Master took a walk out in nature, usually by himself. He loved the quiet time. He loved the safe space that a walk provided him, for it was a space where he could open up to nature and all of the interdimensional energies.

He loved this also as a time of rebalancing, because even though he was a Master, the energies of the planet and other people, and sometimes even his own past affected him, throwing him off balance and bringing him back into limitation. During these solitary evening walks, when he could feel the ground beneath his feet and the air upon his skin, he allowed himself to rebalance.

However, on this particular day, he decided to invite one of his students to come along with him. He had been keeping an eye on Christina lately because he could see that she was having challenges. This experience of moving into embodied enlightenment was very difficult for her, and the Master could see that she had come to a point of getting very stuck.

This often happens with those who are on the path to enlightenment, and it can be overwhelming. Sometimes, they get so caught in their own perceptions that the energy tends to freeze up. It simply doesn't move, and then the student tries to get out of the stuck energies using stuck energy itself, which of course only makes everything worse. And that's exactly what the Master had noticed lately with Christina.

So, he invited her out for a walk on this particular evening. As they walked along, she started to cry and finally said, "Oh Master, why is it so difficult? I know in my heart I've chosen enlightenment. I am so committed to it, but it is so hard in many ways. There are days when I don't think I can go any further; when I think I must have missed something. I don't feel the ease and grace that the other students seem to have. Is it because my past is so heavy? Is it because I am weak and lack insight? Dear Master, what am I doing wrong? Why do I feel so stuck? Why do I feel like I want to escape but have no place to escape to? I want to go back to the time long before I ever embarked on this path of enlightenment, because in a way it was easier back then. Everything was simpler. I didn't have all these overwhelming sensitivities and thoughts and feelings. But of course, I know I can't go back, so I feel utterly trapped." She sniffled a bit.

The Master walked on in silence, breathing the air and feeling into Christina's dilemma. Finally, he said, "Dear Christina, let me tell you the story of the Land of Blue." Christina listened through her tears as the Master began telling the story.

\* \* \*

The Land of Blue wasn't always blue. In the very beginning, it was the Land of Light and included all colors – white, yellow, orange, red, violet, blue – even colors that you could never perceive through the human eye. All colors were there, but the most treasured of colors was blue, particularly a vivid, brilliant electric blue.

As time passed and many, many generations came and went, there were those who sought blue above all other colors. They worshipped blue, and some were able to bring more blue into their life than others. Blue became the color of power, wealth and intelligence. Blue became the elite color in the Land of Light, to the point that all people began to seek and desire nothing but blue.

Finally, with so much focus on blue over so many generations, everything in the Land of Light was now only blue. Gone were gold and pink and green and all the other colors of the spectrum, for everything in this land was now blue. The trees were blue. The ground was blue. The food was blue and people were blue. Of course, now that blue was so important, the sky became blue because it was above everything, and the water also became blue because it was such an important element to life itself.

Now, there were different shades and hues of blue, but at the core, everything in the Land of Light had now become blue. There were people who now accumulated and hoarded blue, who kept the highest levels of blue away from other people. There were those who used the electric vibrant blue for their currency, wealth and power. All the land had turned blue.

Many more generations passed and now it was simply assumed that everything was blue. The people no longer had any memory that there had ever been any other colors, for all they knew was blue. Life went on like this for a long time within what was now the Land of Blue. Blue was used for barter and for power, even as a form of energy. It was all blue.

At a certain point, there was a small number of people scattered throughout the land who began feeling uneasy and uncomfortable. They felt something wasn't right, but they didn't know what it was. They felt impatient, aggravated, even rebellious, but they had no understanding of why they felt this way. Others told these people that there must be something a little bit wrong with them; that they should be satisfied with the blue that they had, even if it wasn't much; that they should stop looking for something else and just try to fit in to blue. When they talked to others about their anxiety, they were told, "You just have to make blue work better for you. That's the whole key to being here in this Land of Blue. It's all about blue. Just be happy with it and stop fighting it. Stop turning against it. Just be more blue, that's all you need."

These people tried very hard to fit in to blue. They joined blue enhancement groups and blue therapy groups. They tried to focus on acquiring more of the brilliant electric blue. They tried to make blue a bigger part of their life, but at the core they were still unhappy. They thought something was wrong with them. They felt odd and different, and looked down on themselves for it.

These few people in the Land of Blue were actually feeling into the fact that there was something much, much more. They tried to figure out what that 'more' was, but they were using blue books, reading blue literature and seeking blue advice, none of which could help them at all. They tried praying to blue. They went to blue gurus and blue healers, trying to figure out what was wrong, but nothing helped.

The problem was that they intuitively knew there was something more, much more, and they were right. Part of them remembered back to the time of the Land of Light when there was gold and green, crimson and violet and all the other colors, even white and black. They were not only feeling what had existed before in the Land of Light; *they were also feeling what was still there.* Even though everything was now immersed in blue, in reality it wasn't only blue. People had become so focused blue that they had reduced their spectrum awareness, their ability to sense and feel anything beyond blue. So, even though all the other colors were still around them, everyone was trapped in blue and could perceive nothing else.

These color rebels knew there was something more. They could feel it; they just didn't know how to tap into it. And when they tried to immerse themselves in blue and make blue be the satisfactory color, they felt even worse.

* * *

"Dear Christina," the Master said, "This is much like you. We are both in a Land of Blue right now as we're out on this beautiful evening walk. It means that society and humans have gotten so trapped in their own limitation, so focused on a few elements that are only part of the truth but not the whole truth, that it's almost impossible to get out, because humans right now are using tools from within their prison to try to get out of it. They are just like the people in the Land of Blue who were trying to use blue to get out of blue. It simply doesn't work."

At this point, Christina stopped and looked down at the ground in a moment of contemplation. Then she said, "Master, I feel what you are talking about. I feel that I am trapped in something, but I don't know what it is. Like you said, I have been trying to use tools and methods from within this trap to try to get out of it. But how can I possibly know what is outside? I've tried everything but how can I possibly break out? How can I become free like you are?"

The Master took a good deep breath and said, "Dear Christina, it's about allowing yourself to recognize what your blue is."

"It's quite simple," he continued. "The blue here on the planet is actually the element of time, and humans have gotten deeply stuck and trapped in it. In the beginning, time was an element that allowed the angels on Earth to experience yet another quality of sensuality and dimensionality. But then they got stuck in time; in routines, patterns and processes. As humans, they eventually came to believe that they were the ones moving through time, when indeed the opposite has always been true: Time responds to and moves through consciousness. And at everyone's core is just that – consciousness.

"Money isn't causing humans to do what they do; it's actually time. And you've become part of that. Time created the mind, which then works within the confines of time. In fact, the mind knows nothing *but* time. It cannot possibly imagine going beyond time, just as those people in the Land of Blue could not imagine anything beyond blue. But when you use your mind, which is a construct of time, to try to get out of time, instead it only intensifies, making time deeper, thicker and more difficult to get out of.

"First, dear one, recognize that it is the element of time in which you are stuck, and then recognize that this is not your natural state of being. In other words, you cannot possibly stay in this state forever.

You can have deep and long adventures in time, but you cannot possibly stay trapped in it. There are certain things that people could do in the Land of Blue to prolong their existence in blue, or that you can do to prolong your time within time. But it is an unnatural state, and once you recognize that, it begins to free you.

"What can you do? In a way, the answer is *nothing*. Or, said differently, it is to get out of your own way. Stop trying to fight blue with blue. Stop trying to break out of blue by using blue tools. Take a deep breath and realize that this is not your natural state of being. It was an experience, a very sensual experience, but now tap into your feeling that there's something more, because there is. Tap into the *I Exist*, because that's the very thing that's telling you there is so much more than time. There's so much more than blue.

"As you tap into the consciousness of 'I Exist,' you realize 'I Am that I Am. I'm not time and I'm not blue. I'm not human and I'm not limited.' And, as you truly allow yourself to feel deeply into the 'I Exist,' the 'I Am that I Am,' then you will get another knowingness – '*I Know that I Know*.' This will validate your feelings that there is so much more. The 'I Know that I Know' reminds you that, indeed, you *do* know and you always *have* known. You've been very hard on yourself, wondering what's wrong with you, but there's nothing wrong. You just *know* that there is more than living in the Land of Blue or in the Land of Time.

"When you take a deep breath and feel into the 'I Know that I Know,' you'll realize it's not the mind just trying to create another linear time sequence for you. You'll realize that you *know* there's so much more, and it's right here. And then, simply step out of your old time-filled way and allow the natural evolution, the natural return to yourself to happen.

"At times it's going to be uncomfortable, because there is a part of you that's deeply immersed in the mental time-based reality. You have to be willing to accept that whatever happens in your life now is releasing you from the limitations of the mind and of time itself. When things come along that your time-based self is uncomfortable with or that causes fear and panic, it's important that you take a deep breath and simply *allow* it.

"This applies to everything. Whether it's interactions with other people or experiences in your own life, whether the mind considers it to be good or bad, it doesn't matter. It is about coming to such a point of trust in yourself that you allow the natural evolution beyond the mind and beyond time to take place, to the point where you simultaneously live within time-based reality and are also aware of living within other realities as well. These other realities aren't far away. It is only the mind that sees them at a distance. These other realities are right here, right now. I can see them. They're already part of you, but they're simply not recognized by the spectrum within which your mind functions.

"It's simply taking a deep breath from the 'I Exist' into the 'I Am' into the 'I Know that I Know' and allowing yourself to shift into timeless while also being within time. It feels a little uncomfortable at first, because suddenly there is no past or future; everything is right in the Now. There's no more past to hang on to and claim as yours, because there is no past when you're timeless. There is no more planning and plotting for the future, because in timelessness there is no future. It's all in the Now. That's when you have another liberating realization: 'I Am Here.' And 'Here' is wherever you choose to be. Never again stuck in Blue or in Time.

"Each day may be different, and it may get to the point where you forget what day it is or even where on the planet you live – and it doesn't matter. You have to be willing to let go of things that have been the foundations for your linear, time-based, very blue life. In fact, letting go is all that's required from you.

"It is important to understand that it's not even you – this blue, time-based human – who has the responsibly to get out of time and into enlightenment. Please recognize that it's not up to you. The full You, the Free Self, is not expecting you to do it. As a matter of fact, your Free Self is asking you to stop trying, because you're just using blue to try to get out of blue, and it will never work! Your true consciousness, your Free Self, wants to put its arms around you, hold you close and say, 'Stop trying so hard to get out of blue. I'm already here. We are already here, beyond time and beyond the mind. Stop trying to figure all of this out and simply Allow.'

"If you would listen carefully, dear Christina, you would hear the part of you that's *not* trapped in time, *not* trapped in linear, *not* trapped in the mind, saying to you, 'Let go and know that I am here. Allow the natural return to the light, to all that I Am and that you are. All is well in *all* of our creations.'"

"Dear Christina," the Master continued, "Stop trying to figure it out. Take my hand for a moment, close your eyes, and I'll convey to you what it feels like to go beyond blue without even trying. I'll convey to you here, as you hold my hand, what it feels like to be in blue and out of blue, to be in the mind and out of the mind, to be in time and out of time. I can be here taking a walk in the evening, being very much in time-based reality, but I'm not limited to it. I can shift. I can play with it. I can be within time and this physical reality, and I can also be totally out of time where it's not even a part of my awareness. Most of the time, I'm fully aware of being within time and also outside of it.

"The reality is that you go *beyond*, and what's beyond is nothing like this physical, time-based reality. Beyond is beautiful, and by opening yourself and allowing it to come to be, perhaps you'll realize how beautiful this time- and mind-based reality is, and also that you're no longer limited to it.

"So, dear Christina, our walk has come to an end. Go back and be with yourself. Allow yourself to stop fighting with everything and realize that enlightenment is truly natural. As the blue, time-based human being, it's not your responsibility to get it right. The only thing being asked of you is to Allow. Allow the divine, allow the light of your Self to expand into your reality."

As Christina walked away, she could feel her blues dissolve away and she even had a slight smile. The Master observed all of this and knew it was her smile of coming freedom.

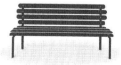

# Story 4

# The Locket

*Inspired by the large rock that rolled down the mountain*
*and hit Geoffrey's car...*

The student, preparing for a long journey, went to see the Master before leaving. "Master," he said, "It will be many months before I return. Do you have any sage advice before I go on my journey?"

The Master opened a drawer, took out a small locket, handed it to the student and said, "Carry it with you but don't open it until you absolutely desperately need it. Not a moment before."

The student took the locket with excitement, thanked the Master and departed. Setting out on his journey he thought, "Ah! This must be a magic elixir the Master has given me, or some secret formula, perhaps a powder that will do magical things!" He was tempted to open the locket and peek inside, but he remembered the Master's words and thought better. So it remained in his pocket as he continued on his journey, until it was almost forgotten.

One day as he was walking through a deep valley surrounded by tall, steep hills, he suddenly heard a noise. It almost sounded like thunder in the sky above the mountains, but when he looked up to check for rain, he saw a huge boulder tumbling down the side of the mountain, headed straight for where he was standing. There was nowhere to hide and he realized it meant impending death, for even if he tried to jump out of the way it was too big and there wasn't enough time.

Suddenly he remembered the locket and, with the boulder now just a few meters away, he quickly pulled it out and opened it. He hoped there would be some magic formula to save him, but instead found only two words etched into the locket: "I Exist."

There was a flash of disappointment but then the student took a deep breath and went to his knowingness. He felt his own Self, his own *I Exist*. And suddenly he was walking down the path with a huge boulder smashed to bits behind him. He was amazed. "I should have been killed! I should be as flat as a pancake, smashed under that boulder. It was so close I could almost touch it. What happened?" And then he remembered, "Ah, *I Exist!*"

You see, that simple consciousness changes the very nature of reality. The very moment he felt into "I Exist" – reminded by looking at the Master's locket and the boulder rushing toward him – he changed the very nature of time itself so that he wasn't in the path beneath the boulder but rather on the path ahead of it. And in fact, both potentials were true; the boulder crushed him *and* he just missed being flattened.

He took a deep breath of Realization and thought, "Ah, I understand! The true nature of reality is that both potentials occurred. I just happened to choose the one where I didn't get smashed into bits." And he joyfully continued on his journey singing "I Exist! I Exist! I Exist!"

\* \* \*

Dear reader, in a way, this can be your story. You're on a journey when suddenly something unexpected comes into your life, perhaps an accident. And, just like the student who carried the locket with him, at the moment of impending disaster you remember "*I Exist.*" That's all it takes. You don't need a magic potion or fairy dust, only to simply know "I Exist." It brings you back to your center, back to your consciousness. It is consciousness that creates everything and consciousness that can change everything. It is the *I Exist.*

The moment you step into your life *in consciousness* – without any games, without any makyo, without forcing anything; simply with the I Exist and the Allowing – it suddenly changes a situation. It can make a quantum change in a health situation, a financial situation or a personal relationship. With the consciousness of "I Exist," suddenly, everything can shift.

You don't try to change the world around you; you shift *yourself* into a different potential. The old potential of the rock crushing the student was still there, but it was not actualized. He literally shifted time through his urgent choice of Allowing and found himself about 22 seconds ahead of the falling rock. What he thought was going to be a disaster was shifted into a type of parallel reality and the rock fell behind him. Both potentials are true. Both existed. One was realized on this level.

Your life can be like that. You don't have to plan or worry about it; it just happens. And when it happens, don't try to go back and try to figure out exactly how it happened; don't go back into the linear mindset. Take a deep breath and just Allow that it happened.

Bring your "I Exist" with you, keep it with you on every step of your journey. Feel it. Live it, and then watch how the very nature of reality and synchronicity change in your life.

# Story 5

# Shortcuts

*Based on several true stories of makyo...*

It was a beautiful, sunny day and Daniel found the Master outside the school's workshop, building a birdhouse. He had a passion for building birdhouses and birdfeeders out of beautiful local wood, and he did it with great care and passion. As he worked, the Master could almost see and feel the birds that would come to enjoy his creations. He loved the touch and feel of the wood, and the creative process of building each birdhouse the old-fashioned way – by hand.

Daniel approached and said, "Master, I found something I'm very excited about! In fact, I think it should be shared with all the students here at the School." The Master looked up from sanding a piece of wood. "And what would that be, Daniel?"

Daniel replied, "I have discovered a substance called ayahuasca. It comes from a vine that grows in South America and is brewed into a tea. Then, when one drinks this beautiful substance, it brings about an amazing spiritual experience that makes them feel very close to God and even to themselves. I've used this substance twice now, and in all of my years here in the School, I've never experienced anything quite like it. It's an amazing opening!"

The Master took a deep breath and smiled to himself. "Yes, Daniel, I am familiar with ayahuasca, for indeed, in my younger days, I participated in some of the sacred ceremonies with the shamans. I've also smoked marijuana and taken a few other things, for in my early days I, much like you, was very, very impatient. I wanted to push the whole process of opening my consciousness and expanding into the other realms. So, yes, indeed, I'm very familiar with what you're talking about."

Daniel said, "Wonderful! So you understand why I'm suggesting that we do this sacred ceremony with the students here at the School." The Master stood up and faced Daniel directly. "My dear friend, I said I was familiar with it, but I didn't say that I was currently using any such substance. And it's not something that we're going to do with the students, for here at this Mystery School it's about the *natural* way to enlightenment."

Daniel was quite surprised. He had thought the Master would at least want to use it for himself or even do a sacred ceremony with a few of the students. He said, "But Master, if a totally natural substance like ayahuasca truly opens you up quickly, why wouldn't you want to do it here at the school? Isn't it all about discovering the mysteries?"

"Daniel," the Master said, "This is not something that I would recommend to anyone on a true and committed spiritual path. I understand when you say it provides a very fast opening of consciousness and an amazing experience, but I have a question for you. How do you feel now that you've tried this a few times?"

"Oh, I feel so open," said Daniel. "The experiences were absolutely amazing. I've never felt anything quite like it. Even in all my years of yoga and meditation, I've never had anything like that. I can't wait to do it again. And of course, Master, I always do it with a shaman. I don't just do it on my own. It's not done for the sake of partying or distraction or anything else like that. It's a very, very sacred ceremony. So I don't understand why you wouldn't want to do it here at the school."

The Master looked very deeply into Daniel eyes and said, "But how do you feel *right now*? It's obvious that you're not in the middle of one of these induced experiences. How do you feel right now as we stand here?"

Daniel took a deep breath and thought for a moment. "Well, I feel excited and can't wait to get back into that experience again. I've had two so far, and I'm thinking that after a few more, I'll have a total opening, a total integration and the ultimate spiritual experience."

"Daniel," the Master said, "What you do is entirely up to you, but we're not going to introduce it here at the school." "Well, you always talk about being free, following our heart and making our own choices," replied Daniel. "So, dear Master, it is something I'm going to continue." And with that, he gave the Master a perfunctory hug and walked away.

About a month later, and more than five years after he had joined, Daniel quit the Mystery School. He had been a good student, although he was always impatient, always wanting to push and go faster. He had met with the Master many, many times and talked about his desire to open *now*, to realize *now*, and he got frustrated when things seemed to be going slow or he didn't feel himself making any progress. So the Master wasn't terribly surprised when he learned that Daniel had quit.

Two years later, the Master met Daniel once again. The Master was at the local farmer's market where the School took much of its produce from the garden to sell to the community. It was a very enjoyable activity and also very profitable for the school, because the things they grew – vegetables, fruit, berries, many types of flowers – all had such a life force energy that the locals bought them as fast as the School could grow them. The vegetables were larger than at any of the other stalls, and the people who came to buy every week found them to be extremely flavorful and delicious. Of course, everything was grown naturally and organically, but that wasn't the only thing that made the difference. It was the energy and consciousness of each and every student who worked in the gardens, adding their essence to the beautiful things that were grown.

So it was here two years later that the Master once again encountered Daniel. He was shopping in the market, and when the Master saw him walking through the stalls, he called him over. "Daniel! Let's chat for a moment."

They left the stall, walked over to a bench near the river, and sat down to talk. The Master took a quick feel of Daniel's energy and asked, "How are you doing, my friend?"

Daniel took a deep breath and sighed. "I took many, many journeys with the shamans and ayahuasca, but I was disappointed to find that while the experiences were expansive, I couldn't seem to integrate them back into my daily life. I would have these amazing sacred journeys into the other realms, into the feeling of wholeness and oneness, into what felt like being in the presence of God and even my own spirit. But every time I came back from one of these journeys, life itself seemed even more difficult. I got frustrated with day-to-day human life and became very depressed. I had access to two worlds, but never at the same time. Sometimes I was in the world of these sacred journeys, but then I always came back to the mundane human world. It got to the point where I wanted to be in these ayahuasca journeys all the time and it was making me ill. I felt burned out, like I wasn't part of life anymore, so I finally stopped.

"I walked away from that group and their shamans, and haven't done one of those journeys for about six months. But now, just a few weeks ago, I found something truly amazing! Have you ever heard of a water immersion journey? It's very good for cleansing and healing my body, and is a very sacred experience. The group I joined has a special system that gives us air while we're underwater, and we allow ourselves to be immersed for hours and hours at a time. It's supposed to cleanse the body, bring us back to our roots and keep all of our energies balanced."

The Master looked at Daniel with curiosity and asked, "And how are you feeling with that?" "Well," Daniel said, "I feel it has cleansed my system, to a large degree, from all those ayahuasca journeys. And, if I continue this immersion therapy, I'm sure it will soon bring all my energy and essence back together. And I'm sure this will help me break through into my enlightenment."

"Well, dear Daniel," the Master said, "You're always welcome to come back to the School at any time. As you know, there are those who come and then leave, and there are many who actually return. It's often important for them to go off on their own journey to experience and try out different things, because many of the students get impatient and try to push their enlightenment. But I have to tell you, Daniel, if you do come back to the school, there's one small prerequisite."

"What is that, Master?" Daniel asked. "Because I actually have been thinking about coming back."

The Master said, "If you come back, you must let go of all these other therapies and treatments. I want you to come back as yourself, not involved in any type of healing or therapy program, not even things like yoga. Nothing. If you come back, come back just as yourself."

Daniel stared at the ground for a while. He thought about what it would be like to return to the Mystery School, which had provided him with so many insights, so much comfort and so much safety. At last he looked up and said, "Thank you, dear Master, for your offer. I will think about it."

It was time for the Master to get back to selling the fruits and vegetables from the School garden, something he loved nearly as much as he loved building birdhouses. They stood up and hugged. It was the last time the Master ever saw Daniel.

\* \* \*

Dear friend, on the road to enlightenment it is very likely that you're going to get impatient, thinking that you're not moving fast enough, that you're trapped and unable to break through. You're going to blame it on mass consciousness or your own lack of ability or simply your humanness. You will look for things to speed it up, whether ayahuasca, marijuana, immersion therapies, crystal therapies or anything else. One way or another, you will get to a point of impatience.

The impatience comes because you can feel the impending enlightenment, the looming Realization. You can feel that you're so close, almost ready to break through, but yet something pushes you back every time. That pushing back is often caused by your own doubts, which are natural. It also happens because there are still unintegrated aspects of yourself; the ones that are still dissociated from you, the ones that haven't felt the full level of Allowing or harmony or trust from you to yourself. These are the things that are holding you back, but these are also the things that cannot be overcome by any therapy, medication, drug, sacred ceremony or anything else outside yourself.

These aspects that have not come back into balance, that have not been integrated back into you, are simply waiting to know that you are at a point of love and trust in yourself. They are waiting for you to be at a point of total Allowing, without any gimmicks, games or external therapies. There is not a single therapy, substance or group in the whole world that can bring you your enlightenment, but it's very seductive to think that there is. It's very seductive to think that, by taking some sort of sacred herbal remedy, you're suddenly going to break through.

Yes, these things can provide a temporary type of breakthrough, a temporary opening of consciousness. But, as Daniel discovered, even though there was an opening into the other realms, it is not integrated into the reality of your day-to-day life. It's like living in two separate worlds. With any outside therapy, no matter what it is, you'll find that this very seductive energy will give you a temporary breakthrough, but then it will cause an even greater degree of anxiety, impatience and, ultimately, depression. This is because you go into an altered and often very beautiful state, but yet you are unable to integrate that and sustain it in your regular world. You'll begin to loathe the everyday human life and want to escape from it, and that's not what we're here to do.

What we're doing is embodied enlightenment, which means the whole self becomes fully integrated into your everyday life, integrated into this world that you helped to create, and into the reality of this planet that you helped to architect. We're allowing the full integration of the physical body, the mind and the spirit all together. We're not trying to run from it nor are we trying to break down the door of enlightenment, as Daniel was doing. Rather, we are allowing the natural, smooth and graceful integration of every part of self.

I know there are times when you feel you're not making any progress, but that's a human judgment. I know there are times when you feel that you're actually going backwards, but you simply can't. And there are times when you feel that some sort of outside stimulus, therapy or program will help you break through, but ultimately it won't.

Daniel did indeed go into realms of expanded consciousness – some were very real and some were more hallucinated, not quite so real – but it is what I would call an unnatural route. He was trying to break through, but he had disregarded many of his own aspects that still needed to be integrated.

The way to enlightenment is absolutely natural. It is about the integration of every part of yourself and, ultimately, it is about Allowing. It is not about a grand angel or your divinity coming in from some far off dimension or planet to rescue you, for that is placing it outside of you. Enlightenment is already there. It's already within.

Story 6

# The Christmas Tree

*Inspired by an actual falling human…*

It was Christmastime, Harold's favorite time of the year. He loved the holiday season so much and that morning he decided to do the final decorations on the huge Christmas tree in the grand hall of the spiritual school. He came in before any of the other students had even awakened so he could put the finishing touches on a tree that was almost seven meters tall.

Harold pulled out the huge ladder, the decorations, ornaments and lights, and assembled them around the tree. Then he started up the ladder holding the tree topper; a beautiful, crystal angel that would be put high atop the tree.

Just as he was reaching to put the angel in place on the top branch, he heard the door open and turned around to see the Master come in. And in that early morning moment of looking over to see the Master, you can guess what happened to poor Harold. He lost his balance, tumbled down the ladder and landed on the crates of ornaments on the floor, broke his arm and two ribs, cut his face on one of the glass ornaments and passed out.

The Master stood watching all this from the back of the room. He didn't feel bad for Harold, but rather understood that it was actually perfect. Now the Master walked over to where Harold's body laid limp, still holding the crystal angel that was meant as a tree topper (which was now partially broken with bits of it in his face), looked at the blood streaming down Harold's face, took a deep breath, pulled out his smart phone and called for an ambulance.

A few hours later the Master was at the hospital, standing beside the bed of poor Harold, whose arm was now in a cast, who was in great pain from the broken ribs and who had a large bandage covering the many stitches on his forehead. Harold woke up when the Master came into the room, and now the Master said, "So, dear Harold, what were you thinking? What was going through your mind when you fell off the ladder?"

Harold pondered for a moment, thinking back to the incident and said, "Well, Master, there were two main things. The first thought was, 'Am I going to live? It's a long way down, there are a lot of boxes on the ground, and I'm not a youngster anymore. Am I going to live?'"

"Yes," the Master said, "And what else?"

Harold answered, "You know, alone in that room to decorate the tree, I was thinking about my life. It's a good one; I'm married to a wonderful partner, I have two great children and a nice house. But what have I really done? I've been involved in this spiritual community for the last five years, but what have I really accomplished? Am I just distracting myself? Have I really learned anything or am I just spinning my wheels? Is it all a distraction from a life that I might otherwise be bored with? That's what I was thinking."

"Perfect," the Master said. "Absolutely perfect. You know, when these things happen, when you have a fall or an accident, always go back to what was going through your mind at the time. You were decorating the tree for the holidays, thinking about your life and wondering if you've done a good job in your spiritual quest. You were thinking about your own commitment, whether you were being honest and true to yourself, and suddenly everything went out of balance. It wasn't because I walked in that you fell out of balance. I walked in *because* you were out of balance. I was the perfect distraction, the perfect reason for you to turn around on the ladder, lose your balance and fall off. And, in doing so, it caused you to wonder 'Am I really alive?' Here you are now, in the hospital, probably thankful that it wasn't worse and that there is no permanent damage. You'll heal quickly, but it made you consider your life."

"People are interesting," the Master continued. "More than anything else they want to feel alive, but they don't always know how to. And then they do strange things to make themselves feel alive, like falling off a ladder. You may have thought it was some sign from God or the universe, but it wasn't. It was a way for you to feel alive. And certainly, by beckoning death, you did indeed feel alive. Being in pain, as you are right now, actually reminds you that you're alive. Pain is funny like that. While it is very difficult and, well, painful, it does remind you that you're alive.

"Why is it that humans sometimes do insidious and painful things just to make themselves feel alive? Why is it that humans will drive down the freeway at incredible, even frightening speeds? It's all for the thrill of feeling alive! Why is it that humans turn up the music so loud that their ears can barely tolerate the noise? Because that noise and vibration, that external power and energy coming in through their ears, makes them feel alive.

"Why is it that humans argue with other people, even the ones they love most? Because it makes them feel alive. Yes, Harold, even an argument makes you feel alive. It gets something going in what might be an otherwise boring life. It gets some energy moving in a life so monotonous one begins to wonder if they're really alive, if they're really worthwhile, if they're really doing anything of value. Why do humans play extreme games? Why do some humans hurt themselves intentionally? Why do humans take drugs or drink to excess, Harold? Because it makes them feel alive.

"There are, indeed, better ways to feel alive, but very few humans realize that. So they resort to these external challenges. They do strange, extreme things just to feel alive, because there is truly nothing worse than feeling dead, numb and worthless, even though you still have a physical body. So they do whatever they can to feel alive.

"Harold, in a way, your fall from the ladder was answering a question to yourself: 'Am I really alive?' Am I doing anything significant in my life?' And – the real question – 'Am I letting myself *feel* life? Or am I closing it off and compromising? Am I always trying to satisfy other people and give to others first?' You can't feel alive that way. As a matter of fact, when you're always putting others first, each day you'll feel a little bit more dead, because they're taking energy from you and you are allowing them to do it. When you fell off that ladder and then passed out from the excruciating pain, it actually made you feel very alive. Isn't that strange?" the Master asked.

"Harold, I've known you for five years. You've been a good student, but you doubt and question yourself, and hold yourself back. You still feel that it's important to do everything for everyone else, that you have to help everyone else be happy. You still limit yourself. You still feel ashamed to have more in your life than someone else. In a way, you're killing yourself slowly, day by day. Oh, you tell yourself that you're a good father and a good husband; you have a good job and no debt. But you know as well as I do that you really haven't been feeling very much alive."

At that point, Harold broke down in tears. He knew exactly what the Master was talking about. It actually felt very good to let himself cry. The Master did not try to counsel him or pat him on the shoulder and say "Everything is going to be all right," because he knew this moment of crying was allowing Harold to truly feel alive again. He knew that, as these emotions and tears of release came out, Harold was opening up to his soul.

At that very moment, the door opened and in came a group of volunteer holiday carolers. They began to sing a beautiful Christmas song, and the Master said, "Hark, oh Harold, the angels sing!" And Harold groaned, not from the pain of his injuries but from the pain of the Master's bad sense of humor.

* * *

Dear reader, I can tell you that life will only get more intense, and that's good because you're going to feel more alive. There is no room in your life anymore to just get by. Now it is truly a question of whether to barely survive or to be fully alive. There's no more middle ground, no more holding back.

Surviving isn't very fun, is it? You didn't come here to survive, and that's part of the conflict. That's what makes you different from other people, because you will not tolerate just surviving. You will fall off of a very tall metaphorical ladder if you're just surviving from now on, for you won't let yourself live that way.

The Master didn't make Harold fall off that ladder; Harold caused himself to fall. The Master just happened to walk in the room at the perfect time. It was Harold's knowingness gnawing at him, a knowingness that he was just getting by, that there was more, but also feeling that he was suppressing it. He wanted to be a good father, a good husband, a good student, a good everything, and it just wasn't working anymore. He was only surviving; he wasn't really alive.

The greatest thing for a souled being is to know the I Am, and that means to truly feel alive. You came to this planet to embody in biology, to *experience life,* and there is no better way to feel alive than to have five human senses, a physical body that can experience pleasure and pain, and to be in a linear reality with all of its narrowness and focus. But, at a certain point, you get caught in the routines and ruts, in mass consciousness and programming, in your own dogma and energetic filth, and you come to a stop. You compromise. You hold back.

You say you want the enlightenment? Enlightenment can be easy *if* you don't get in your own way. When life comes to you, embrace it. Command it. Dance with it. Experience it. *Feel alive* with it.

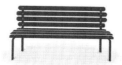

# Story 7

# The Clock Tower

*Inspired by those who exist in* and...

The Master was out for an evening stroll when he encountered a student in the town square just as the clock tower struck seven o'clock. "Master, what a coincidence!" the student cried. "I was just thinking about you and suddenly here you are."

The Master smiled and said, "It's not a coincidence at all, for I'm not only here. Indeed, at this hour of seven o'clock in the evening I'm back at my house cooking a delicious dinner. I just opened a bottle of wine and am enjoying the very best that life has to offer. Yet, at the same time, I am also here with you beneath this clock tower, because at the moment you thought about me, I became reality in both places at once."

The student was amazed. He stood for a moment looking at the Master, wondering what it would feel like to be in more than one place at the same time; not just a wispy ghost, but fully embodied, conscious, aware and very present. Finally, the student asked, "Master, I would love to hear more about how you're able to do this, but right now I'm on my way to a spiritual meeting. Could we meet tomorrow evening to talk about it?"

\* \* \*

Dear reader, some of these very simple truths are right there for you to behold. But when you're in the consciousness and limitations of time; when you're so busy trying to figure out how to fit into time and make your current reality better, even though the answer is right in front of you, it's almost invisible. You're so immersed in time – in schedules, plans and programs – that you walk right past the answer you're seeking, just as the student did with the Master.

You're accustomed to singular reality, singular thought and, definitely, singular consciousness. It requires a whole lot of work on your part to even let yourself imagine outside of singular consciousness. When I say there are realities all around us that go beyond the physical nature of this universe, you think about it, but you just think of another universe with the same types of galaxies and stars and everything else that we have here. It's not like that at all.

Once you leave this perspective or plane of consciousness that includes time and space, it all changes. And, when you coexist outside of time and space, the consciousness is not just singular, not just in one point of Time-Space; it is plural, very multidimensional. Your consciousness can be in many places or it can be in one, as it was with the Master standing at the clock tower with the student *and* simultaneously cooking a meal back at home. This is not science fiction or some magical dream. This is the way reality is supposed to be.

Now, it's usually easier to be in this Time-Space continuum and also at a point *outside* of time and space. But if you allow yourself, you'll be able to literally coexist in multiple locations and multiple points of consciousness *within* this time and space continuum. You can do it just by choice. The fact is that you can be here *and* there. You don't leave time and space to go off and exist in some other realm; you coexist in both.

The bottom line is that the human self wakes up and starts to recognize that it is part of a multidimensional being that's not stuck in time and space. The human self realizes that it can continue to be in time and space, in the physical world, *and* simultaneously be aware of itself and the rest of the being in these other points of consciousness.

In other words, you can experience elements of time, space, physical nature and reality right here, and simultaneously experience what it's like outside of time.

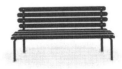

# Story 8

# The Laundromat

*Based on someone we all know...*

The Master had scheduled a meeting with a student by the name of Nicholas. Nicholas had been experiencing a lot of inner chaos and turmoil so the Master agreed to get together with him. He gave Nicholas the address of the meeting place, which happened to be the local Laundromat, where people go to wash their clothes.

The Master loved going to the laundry even when he didn't have any clothes to clean. He would watch the people come in with baskets full of dirty clothes, put them into a machine, add some soap, put their little coins into the slot and then watch the machines go round and round. For the Master, this was one of the most amusing places of all.

The Master arrived promptly at 11 o'clock, dressed for the occasion. He wore an early 20th century golfer outfit, with breeches and long socks, a rumpled cravat and a colorful beret on his head. He had noticed that humans wear some of the oddest clothing when they went to the Laundromat, so he thought he would do so as well.

He sat down to wait and, as he could have guessed, Nicholas was nearly thirty minutes late. It was somewhat irritating for the Master, because you'd expect the student would be on time for such an important meeting.

Eventually Nicholas came stumbling through the door, looking up at the Laundromat sign and checking the address. He wondered if he had the right place, but then noticed the Master sitting off to the side in his colorful and rather unusual attire. He should have wondered why the Master was dressed like that, but Nicholas was mostly unconscious. In other words, he was not really aware of anything, even himself.

Nicholas sat down next to the Master and immediately started making excuses. "I'm so sorry, Master, but the traffic was terrible and I got lost along the way. I meant to be here early to meet you. I'm so sorry." The student went on and on, coming up with a whole list of excuses. The Master knew that Nicholas' life was an absolute wreck. He was always late for everything; because he was so controlled by the dimension of time, it was shaping his life instead of the other way around.

The Master said, "Nicholas, how are you doing today?" Nicholas finally caught his breath, still pretty much unaware that he was in a laundromat or that people all around him were washing their dirty clothes, and said, "Oh, I'm fine, Master. I'm doing fine."

The Master nodded and asked, "And how is that health problem you were dealing with?" Nicholas said, "Oh, it's getting better. I'm really working at it, changing my diet and doing a lot of cleansing. I'm sure it will be gone soon." The Master just listened. He had known Nicholas for a while and Nicholas was always doing some kind of new healing thing, but yet his health problems were persistent.

The Master said, "Nicholas, how's your self-awareness?" This caught Nicholas off guard. He had to stop for a moment. The truth was that there was very little self-awareness, but Nicholas said, "Oh, my self-awareness is getting so much better, and I'm really loving myself. Just like you said in the classes, it's about loving yourself and I really get it!"

The Master listened to all of this, then he said, "Nicholas, you're lying." Now, this really caught Nicholas off guard, because more than anything else he hated being called a liar. His parents had accused him of lying quite a few times, and this went deep. Call him stupid, call him immature, but don't call him a liar. He started having flashbacks of the many times his parents caught him in lies. The Master's accusation really affected him and, as per his habit, he immediately started denying it. "I'm not lying! I really am getting better! My health is getting better. My self-awareness is getting better. I'm more abundant. My whole life is getting better."

The Master said, "Not only are you a liar, you're a skilled and highly proficient liar." Nicholas got very upset, arguing with the Master and going into even more denial. He thought maybe this was just a test the Master was putting him through and he adamantly denied, "No, no, no! My life *is* getting better. I know I'm going to get a job soon, I know this health problem is almost licked, and people are saying that I look more radiant than ever. It's all good!"

But it was all a lie, and the Master knew it. He looked Nicholas straight in the eye, looking right through him, through his lies and deceit. The student tried to keep a brave face but he could feel the Master's gaze looking deep within him, and at last he broke down crying. Right there in the laundromat, with the Master dressed in his early 20th century golfing clothes; right there among the piles of dirty laundry and noisy machines, Nicholas was crying like a little boy.

Now, you would think that the other people doing their laundry would have noticed this, but, like Nicholas, they were asleep as well. They were so numb to everything, including themselves, that they didn't notice this rather unusual scene – a man on the floor crying, another man nearby practicing his golf swing. Such a strange scene, but nobody noticed.

The Master putted patiently until Nicholas was spent. It had been a long time since Nicholas had wept, and it helped to cleanse some of his own inner dirty laundry. It let him realize that he was indeed a liar. Finally, the student got up from the floor, sat back down on the chair and the Master put his golf balls away. The student said, "Master, I am so sorry that I came here today and lied to you. I don't know why I did it and I'm very sorry. Obviously you have great psychic power, for you can see right through my lies."

"I don't care if you lie to me. It doesn't matter one bit," the Master said. "What matters is the lying to yourself. Nicholas, your whole life is one big lie. I'm not talking about the kind of lies that your parents accused you of. The real lie is the lie you tell yourself.

"Your whole life is a lie. Everything you've done up to now is a lie. Your self-perception is nothing but a lie. But, Nicholas, you're not alone in this. You see these other people? Their lives are also lies. People walking down the street, their lives are lies, meaning they are not true, not complete. Nicholas, somewhere deep inside you know your life is a lie and, no matter what you do, you're not going to be happy. No matter how much you try to cover it up or heal it or mend it, no matter how many spiritual classes you take, it's just never going to feel right. And that's the real sadness."

The Master continued, "You know, Nicholas, humans are kind of like this laundromat. They come in with their dirty clothes, add a little detergent, drown them in some water, spin and rinse them, and then dry and fold them. They keep doing that week after week, trying to get a little dirt out of their lives. Week after week, they come in here with soiled garments. Week after week, they go home and put on the same clothes. One would think that, after a while, they would get totally new clothes – totally change themselves – or at least not get their garments dirty in the first place. But week after week, year after year, they come in here to wash, rinse, spin and dry, over and over again.

"That's what human life is like, dear Nicholas. That's what you and so many others have been doing. And then you lie to yourself that you like it, that you're making progress, that you enjoy washing clothes. You lie to yourself about life but you know that it just isn't right. Nicholas, I want you to go home, take off all your clothes and get naked. And don't put those clothes back on until you have truly gotten naked with yourself, in other words until you have allowed yourself to see who you really are, what your life is really about and what you really want. Stop the lies, Nicholas. Stop covering all of this up. Go home and get totally naked with yourself."

Nicholas felt stunned, confused and insulted, but he knew the Master was correct. He gathered his things, still unaware that the Master was dressed in his golfing outfit and everybody else was washing their dirty clothes, went home, and forgot to take off his clothes. Instead, he fell sound asleep on the bed and woke up the next day to the same lies, the same wash, rinse, spin and dry cycles.

So goes the story of the Master; not always a happy ending. Oh, maybe one of these days Nicholas will understand that he's been lying to himself, that he's been in the same patterns and cycles, asking for advice, studying spiritual things, even having access to a Master, but still getting nowhere. Maybe someday he'll realize it's time to come back to himself, time to Allow who he really is.

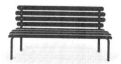

# Story 9

# The Interview

*Inspired by Elvis, the Master...*

Rachel pulled her car into the parking lot of the grocery store, turned off the engine and thought to herself, "What a strange place to have an interview with the Master."

Rachel worked part-time as a bookkeeper, but her real passion was her new spiritual magazine. She loved to communicate and share with others who were awakening and had started the magazine with her own funds. Now she had a tremendous passion for writing the articles every month and had somehow managed to get an interview with the Master. In fact, it had been much easier than she'd expected. She thought he would be very busy and wouldn't have time to waste on an interview with a start-up reporter for a start-up magazine, but indeed he had granted the interview. He almost seemed delighted by it, as if he didn't have anything better to do, almost as if he had been waiting for the call. But how strange, she thought, that the Master would arrange to have the interview at the grocery store.

It was a Saturday morning, one of the worst times to go to a grocery store. The Master had told Rachel to meet him inside and that she would know who he was right away. But she felt a bit confused, bewildered and somewhat nervous about actually being in the presence of a Master. "Can a Master see all of my thoughts?" she wondered. "Perhaps I should ask that question in the interview. But if he can, he'll already know I'm going to ask it. Can the Master see all the bad things I've ever done? Well," she thought with a wry smile, "If he could he probably wouldn't have granted this interview."

Rachel made her way into the store, grabbed a basket out of habit, and looked around for someone who looked like a Master, perhaps somebody dressed in a very elegant robe. Suddenly, she was surprised to see someone dressed up as Elvis, complete with a white polyester leisure suit with wide lapels, a large belt, dark sunglasses and slicked-back hair. Rachel wondered for a moment, "Could that be …? No, of course not." But then she looked again. The Master flashed her a big smile and said, "Man, I really love Vegas." She thought it must all be a big mistake, but it wasn't, for Masters love dressing up in all sorts of ways – Elvis, birds, anything – just because they can. They like to dress a bit different every day so they don't get locked in the same old rut of wearing the same old clothes.

The Master walked over and greeted Rachel, not with the typical "Namaste" as she had expected, but, "Man, I really like Vegas!" Now, this completely threw her off, which of course was part of the Master's whole intention. He wanted to get her out of her comfort zone and all her presupposed conclusions about what was going to happen during this interview, and certainly he had succeeded. Here she was to interview an Elvis impersonator-cum-Master in a grocery store on a crowded Saturday morning. It was already way out of Rachel's comfort zone.

The Master said, "Come, let's walk. I have shopping to do." He grabbed a cart and, as they started making their way through the store, Rachel asked her first question. "Dear Master, my readers are interested in this thing called the New Earth. Where is it?" The Master took a deep breath and said, "It isn't anywhere. And, it's everywhere."

"Is it Planet X?" Rachel asked. The Master said, "No, not really. There are some who feel into the New Earth and give it this title of 'Planet X.' Then it sounds very mysterious and conspiratorial – the strange planet hidden behind the sun or wherever it is – but no, it's not Planet X. That's a beautiful distraction for those who really don't want to understand the New Earth. It's not Nibiru either, this 'lost planet' that some talk about. It is Earth, but it's not physical. It doesn't exist anywhere in particular and it exists everywhere. New Earth is a beautiful point of consciousness."

Rachel, not quite sure where to go next with the question, asked, "Who lives on New Earth?" "Anyone who has the awareness is there," said the Master. "Anyone who understands the beauty of life on this Classic Earth, anyone who's had a dream or a hope of the fulfillment of this Classic Earth, anyone who is choosing their own sovereignty and freedom. It's not a club or something you have to be voted into. New Earth is the hope, the dream, the fulfillment and the completion of this planet."

"When people die, do they go to New Earth?" Rachel asked. "Not necessarily," the Master replied. "When most people die they go to the Near Earth realms, a sort of mass consciousness cloud that surrounds Classic Earth. In fact, most people go exactly where their beliefs lead them to, for whatever they believed on Classic Earth is what they experience in the Near Earth realms. Very few humans actually go to the New Earth, and very, very few truly understand how to be there in consciousness. So, no, it's really not a place where people go between lifetimes."

Now Rachel was even more confused. She had been hoping for very succinct answers for her article, but was having a hard time understanding what the Master was talking about. So she came back to her main question. "But where is this New Earth?"

The Master knew this would be her biggest question and it was the very reason he had invited her to the grocery store. "The New Earth is here," he said. "It's not just in one place; it's everywhere. In a way, it's like this grocery store. You see, as we are walking up and down the aisles of this store, there is an abundance of choices, a tremendous selection the likes of which was unheard of 50 or 100 years ago. Here you can buy everything from lettuce to medications to flowers, fresh bread, tools and detergent. Anything you want is right here.

"The amazing thing is that there is so *much* to choose from. If you are conscious about your body, there are many healthy foods to choose from. There is food fresh from the field, organically grown without pesticides, free of what you call GMO. There is food that is grown naturally and with consciousness that responds and resonates with your body.

"If you're in a different place of consciousness, you can buy canned vegetables, fried foods, even things that were baked months ago and wrapped in plastic. Whatever you want is all here. And the beauty is that you have a choice in it. You can get products of higher consciousness, and even if they cost a little bit more it doesn't really matter to someone of consciousness. Or you can get products that have had the life force energy baked, fried, smashed and processed out of them, products that are more abusive to the environment and to your body. It's all right here.

"It is a wonderful analogy for the New Earth. You're in it right now. It's everywhere around you, all the attributes, the freedom, the expression, the sovereignty, the non-linear, non-intellectual way of being. It's right here on the shelf, right here in your everyday life, but most people don't see it. And that is actually part of the beauty of the New Earth. It's not hidden and there's no conspiracy to keep it away from people. The government certainly does not control it, because government does not exist on New Earth. There's no need for it. The New Earth is right here for the conscious human to behold and take part in, just like this grocery store.

"Do you realize that some of the people here have no understanding of organic food? All they know is that it costs more and doesn't taste as greasy or sugary or salty. When they come into the store to shop, they can only see the types of food that match their consciousness. They are drawn to foods that perhaps have added salt or sugar or flavorings, but that really aren't conducive or harmonious with the light body. They buy things because they're cheap, not because they're the best. They buy things because their parents bought the same things and they simply don't have the consciousness to make a different choice. They buy things because it gives them a short-term burst of energy, such as something filled with carbohydrates and chemicals. They don't comprehend that they can eat foods that are actually much better for their body where they don't have to get a short term burst of energy, because the energy expands and fulfills them absolutely appropriately."

Rachel took a deep breath and said, "Master, if the two Earths coexist together, even though you say others can't see it aren't they still aware at some level that it's here?" The Master answered, "No, not at all. They simply don't see it, and that's the beauty of the New Earth and Classic Earth. The beauty is that you can be in and of the New Earth, and they just won't see you. You can be free, you can be sovereign, you can express, even walk through a grocery store in an Elvis costume, and they won't see you. Did you notice that nobody has even looked twice at me in my Elvis get-up, other than you? That's the beauty of the New Earth. They're just not going to see you.

"In other words, Rachel, I want you to tell your readers to get over the fear that the darkness of the old Classic Earth is going to infiltrate the New Earth. Tell your readers that those who don't have the consciousness simply won't see it and, therefore, they cannot attack it, steal from it or corrupt it. Therefore, we're never again going to repeat the times of Atlantis with the battles and the wars, with the darkness trying to overcome the light, the feminine seeking resolution for her wounds, because the New Earth has been set up where they just won't see it until they're ready.

"Dear Rachel, tell your readers to stop fearing, to stop holding back, to stop keeping it such a secret from themselves, because New Earth is here. It can be experienced, it can be lived, and it can never be taken away. Tell your readers that it doesn't matter whether or not there is some mass convergence of Classic Earth and New Earth, as if we're going to pull them together and *make* them work together. We don't need to. You can be your own New Earth right now."

The Master smiled, took a deep breath and said, "Now, it's time to go home and work on my dance moves."

Minutes later, Rachael heard an announcement come over the store's public address system: "Elvis has left the building." Oddly enough, it seemed that nobody else heard it as they continued to pick groceries off the shelves.

* * *

The attributes of New Earth, dear reader, are such that you can start living it today. You can start realizing it for yourself. I ask you to stop putting it out there somewhere far away or sometime in the future, to stop thinking that you and others are going to try to force the New Earth and the old Classic Earth together. You don't need to. The New Earth will naturally integrate into each awakening human individually, one at a time. It's not a group effort. The New Earth is within you.

The New Earth is the hope, the freedom, the expression and the fulfillment, and it is occurring right now with every thought that you have, every Allowing that you allow. New Earth is becoming part of each person's life individually and, as you allow that, it begins to change the grids and meridians of the physical planet. It changes the magnetic formations of the planet and even affects the gravitational pull and the polarity of the planet. It's not the other way around. It's not that the magnetic or crystalline grids change first and then you adjust to them. The changes you are making and allowing in your life right now are changing everything else.

As you allow your "I Am" and more of your consciousness to be present; as you feel safer to be who you are, whether it's disguised as Elvis or a nun or whoever you happen to be today; as you feel safer and allow this into your life, it brings New Earth closer and closer into your everyday reality. And as this happens, it brings mass consciousness itself to a new level. It brings the potential of New Earth closer for everyone else, but they still have to choose it for themselves.

There is an inherent fear within you that goes back to the times of Atlantis. It is the fear that they're going to see you, and then they will attack you and destroy the very things that you hold precious. But they won't. They can't, because they just don't connect with it or see it. You know exactly what I'm talking about for you've experienced it yourself. You've gone into a grocery store where you might have been shopping for years, and suddenly you see something new on the shelf, a product or tool or type of food. You wonder if they just started carrying it, but in fact it was always there. Your consciousness or resonance just didn't see it before, even though it had always been available.

So it is with New Earth. You don't have to hide anymore. They're just not going to see you, because they're still involved with others of similar consciousness. When I say "they," I'm talking about the people that have put you down, battled you and tried to pull you into a lower consciousness; the people that have laughed at you and scorned you; the people who are trying to hold onto a very old energy on this planet, and they are everywhere. You can see it in your headlines every day – the religious groups, political groups, business groups and others that are trying to hold back. They don't understand terms like "New Earth." They only want to go back to an old way. They hang on to it with such rigidity, rules and beliefs that have no freedom, and they justify it under the banner of God or prophets or whatever else.

You don't need to fear them, because they simply don't see you. They can't take energy from you because they don't see you. They're not interested in you. They prefer battling with those of their own consciousness. You see this in religious wars, and I don't mean just one religion battling against another religion, but also a religion battling within itself. That is where some of the greatest, ugliest and darkest battles have taken place, because they're dealing with ones that are basically in the same consciousness. They're trying to steal energy from each other, trying to gain some kind of power or authority. They really don't care about you, because you're not on the battlefield.

What I'm saying is that it is safe for you to be who you are and to embrace the consciousness of New Earth. You have helped design the energetic architecture of New Earth, beginning way, way back at the end times of Atlantis. You knew there could be a greater hope and a greater dream. You knew there needed to be a place for the fulfillment of your journey into Realized consciousness, and you are among the ones who helped dream it into being. You've gone there, time and time again, between lifetimes and in your dream state at night, helping to create it as the beautiful place that it has become.

Today, there are over 200 New Earth dimensions. They are needed because New Earth is also the waypoint where the angelic beings, the ones that follow after you, come to learn what it's like to be in the physical body as part of their own Realization of their I Am.

Right now, the way things are means that for any souled being to ascend or to Realize their enlightenment or ascend, they must go by way of Classic Earth or New Earth. In order to become fully embodied in themselves, they must experience what it's like to be consciousness, then attract energy, then become fully embodied in that energy in that reality. This is why each and every souled being comes by way of Earth or one of the New Earths on their journey to enlightenment.

New Earth has also become the library of Classic Earth's consciousness. Mass consciousness is a kind of polluted cloud, a compilation of all the thoughts, choices, actions and everything else that has ever happened on this planet. New Earth, on the other hand, is the library. It doesn't contain the facts and figures and memories and timelines like mass consciousness does. New Earth contains the wisdom, the true beauty and the elegance of everything that's happened here. The essence of your journey is in the library of New Earth and there are those who come from all around the omniverse, from all corners of creation, to feel it and begin to understand your experience.

# Story 10

# The Mothership

*Inspired by our intergalactic origins...*

The Master sat in his comfortable chair near the fireplace, sipping his tea. The students were gathered around for their weekly Wednesday evening meeting with the Master, something they all looked forward to because they loved his stories. Indeed, some knew his stories were based on their own personal experiences, even though he never used their real names out of respect for their journeys. After everyone quieted down, the Master took a few moments to breathe with the students and then began his talk:

"Now, the question I'm going to ask all of you – and not give you the answer but allow you to discover for yourself – is this: Are you going to come back for another lifetime? Or better put, are you already having a future life? Interesting, interesting, interesting. I'll give you something to play with.

"Consider that right now, in this very moment, you may have another lifetime going on. It could be very, very different than the lifetime you're currently experiencing. It may not necessarily be the same old human life, but it could be taking place right now. You could have a past life that is occurring at this very moment, and it could be a lot more enlightened than this lifetime.

"Here, in simple terms, is the way I like to put it: The Mothership has landed.

"Imagine a big Mothership, hovering above your reality, and it sent down all the little pod spaceships, which represent all of your lifetimes. The pods fly down to this planet, they land, and out pops a version of you, an aspect of you, and it lives out a lifetime. At the same time, all the other little space pods that came down to Earth are also having their lives.

"The big Mothership, which represents the soul being, is looking down on all these lifetimes taking place and it can see all of them, for it's looking at a timescape, not a timeline. A timescape is curved, circular and has different shapes and sizes. It's not linear like we experience regular human life.

"So the Mothership is looking down on all these lifetimes taking place, realizing, of course, that they aren't happening in a linear fashion. You don't evolve from one lifetime to the next, gaining a little more wisdom each time, like trying to find your stairway to heaven. It doesn't matter, because you might have one of the lifetimes – one of the little space pods that landed and the being got out and wandered around Earth – that's very, very intelligent and wise, and another one that's a drunk, and another one that has intentionally taken on a physical or mental handicap. All of them are going on simultaneously.

"Again, don't think in terms of time or space. Think in terms of a time- and space-scape where all is happening in its entirety. Still with me?" the Master asked his audience. "Kind of. Hmmm.

"Suddenly, the Mothership realizes it's time to land. It's time for the awakening, the beginning of the enlightenment, so the Mothership says, 'I better collect and gather up all of my lifetimes.' And the funny thing is that YOU, in this lifetime – this little space pod that is energetically the closest, the most bonded with the Mothership – is the first to return. This lifetime is the first to integrate with the Mothership and therefore becomes the captain, assuming its place at the helm and calling all the other lifetimes to get back in their space pods and beam up to the Mothership – 'It's time to come home.'

"Then the Mothership beams up all of the past, future and current Lifetimes, brings them all into the Integration Chamber within the Mothership, and then lands as one; all complete, all integrated, all together.

"As it's landing, all of these beings in the Integration Chamber who had been down there in the little pods start talking to each other. 'I had a great lifetime in Egypt. You should have seen. I was a pharaoh!' And another Lifetime says, 'I had a terrible life in England. The food was awful.'

"The Lifetimes compare stories of what they learned and what they did, sharing their wisdom, and the captain at the helm is listening to all of these stories. Then the captain lands the Mothership, opens to door and proclaims, 'I Am!'"

The Master paused and looked at the students gathered around him. "The captain of the Mothership is none other than you. You've been collecting all of your aspects, past lives and future lives." One of the students asked, "Can you have two lifetimes occurring simultaneously?" "Yes, you can," the Master replied. "It's not done that often, but it can absolutely occur. Chances are you probably won't meet that other Lifetime, and if you did, you probably wouldn't like each other. But, yes, it is absolutely possible.

"Now at this point you, the captain of the Mothership, get out of the space ship and start really living and experiencing life. You know that, because you're the Mothership, you can leave any time you want. You know that you're capable of traveling beyond light speed, beyond time, and also be grounded here on this planet.

"It's you now. You experiencing it. You connecting with and feeling the wisdom, the experiences, the essence of all of these Lifetimes, *even if they are in the future.* I know you scratch your head and say, 'But 300 years from now, what am I going to be like?' It doesn't matter. Be it now! Don't wait 300 years, it's here right now. Be it now.

"You can connect with your angelic roots, your starseed roots or whatever else from the ancient times, even from before you came here when that Mothership was flying around in some other galaxy, because everything is contained in that Mothership, including the starseed. You don't need to go out anywhere to get the answers; you're the Mothership."

The students were amazed, the room so quiet you could have heard a pin drop. "Take a good deep breath," said the Master. "Oh, I love moments like this, because I know it challenges you. You start thinking about all these past and future Lifetimes and everything else, and then I can feel when you realize that it doesn't matter, because it's all within right now."

The Master paused for a few minutes while the students took it all in. When he could feel the energy in the room settle down as the students stopped thinking and started feeling, he said, "Take another good deep breath. Let's begin with consciousness, the light, the awareness. It's the *I Exist. I Am.*

"Consciousness is not your body or your mind. It's *You*, the beautiful being that you are, the essence. Feel into consciousness. It's awareness, and it's so beautifully elegantly simple.

"Consciousness is the awareness of the awareness. And, as simple as it is, most humans are not aware of themselves or their awareness. That consciousness, the I Am, can go anywhere; in and out of time, in and out of space, anywhere. Consciousness can never be taken by another. It can never be damaged or destroyed. It is pure consciousness.

"This is what frees you to travel in space, in time and beyond, for consciousness can go anywhere. There are no limits, no physical barriers. It's not slow like the speed of light; it can be *anywhere* the instant that you allow it.

"We're sitting here talking about consciousness and we're also applying it. Many, many years from now physicists will begin to understand the role of consciousness in any creation, but you're beginning to experience it already. We don't have to know the math or the science behind it, it's just consciousness. It makes reality.

"Consciousness, awareness, can go and be anywhere. It can be the Mothership *and* all the little space pods. *And* it's you.

"Now, when you apply your consciousness to your knowingness, then you have Realization. It's the 'aha' moment that Tobias talked about a long time ago. "Aha!" You get it. It's anchored, grounded. You could say that knowingness is like the Mothership. You can apply your consciousness and be there in knowingness, in Realization. Wisdom that was gathered over Lifetimes past and future, wisdom that was brought in before you ever came to Earth, it's all the knowingness, the wisdom of the soul.

"Don't be distracted by thought. Consciousness is feeling, awareness; it doesn't need thoughts, facts and figures. It just is.

"So, in this beautiful safe space, let your consciousness be in the knowingness of your life. Let your consciousness be in the knowingness of your light body. You don't have to know the science or the details; just let your consciousness be in the knowingness of the light body that already exists, that is already walking around on this planet somewhere in some time. Let your consciousness be in that knowingness without force, without pressure, without trying to figure it out, without fear. When you let consciousness be in the knowingness of the light body, Realization follows.

"It doesn't matter if the Realization is right now or later on; it's already Realized. You don't have to beg or force it to come to you; just be in the consciousness of your light body. If you're not sure how to do that, just imagine the light of your I Am flowing, merging and illuminating the non-awareness of your light body. Imagine your consciousness, your light floating right in to the unaware vessel of your light body. Let it flow in, open and illuminate this thing called the light body. And, just like that, you merge consciousness and knowingness together, and Realization follows. It's that simple."

The Master looked around the room, illuminated by nothing more than the fire in the fireplace. The students were deep into the experience of their consciousness. He thought for a moment about the time years ago when he was always in his mind, nearly oblivious to true experience. He knew that many of the students would continue to struggle with their thoughts rather than being in their knowingness. But he also knew that sooner or later they would give up the mental struggle and simply Allow.

Allow. This was one of the most valuable things he had ever learned on his path to mastery. To allow his I Am presence, his soul and spirit, into his human life rather than having his human self try to be spiritual. It took him a long time to learn this, or rather to *Allow* this, but it was the turning point of his life. He smiled as he looked around the room at his students, their eyes closed in deep wonder, knowing that each and every one of them would eventually come to their Realization. There was no doubt about it in the Master's mind, because he also knew that, sooner or later, enlightenment comes naturally to everyone.

Instead of disturbing his students, he quietly got up from his comfortable chair, took his tea and headed off for bed. It had been a long day; now it was his time to be with his own Mothership in his dream-state.

# Recognition

*Inspired by a lot of seekers...*

Henry was a young man, very much into spirituality and enlightenment, but also rather innocent and naïve. He had only been at the Mystery School for a few months, and now he finally had an appointment to come before the Master. Having heard stories about what it was like, he was filled with both anxiety and excitement, because he knew that when the appointment with the Master came, it meant that the student had reached a certain degree of accomplishment at the School.

Now it was time for Henry to approach the Master. He was a bit nervous, of course, but more than anything he was excited. In a way, having your review with the Master was like getting a job assessment or a report card in school.

Henry approached the Master and said, "Master, how am I doing? It's been a few months and I've been working very hard, being diligent with everything here at this Mystery School. Please tell me Master, how am I doing?"

The Master sat back in his masterly way and said, "Student, it is not for me to measure or judge."

Henry was a bit disappointed, because he really wanted an evaluation from the Master. So he took a deep breath, collected his energy and came up with a new way around this. "Master, would you check with my spirit guides and ask them how I'm doing?"

The Master took a deep breath, clenched his jaw a bit and said, "Student, you have no spirit guides. They were with you for many, many lifetimes, but they got bored and left."

Now Henry was getting discouraged as well as disappointed. But, like all students, he was determined, if also a bit naïve. He collected himself once again, took a deep breath and said, "Master, how do the archangels feel that I'm doing?"

The Master sat with his eyes closed for a long time. Finally, shaking his head just slightly, he opened his eyes but kept them lowered and said, "Student, the archangels are all busy, because there are so many humans now who are channeling them. There is no feedback from any of the archangels."

Henry's heart sank. He felt disappointed, discouraged and even distraught. Then he took a very deep breath and thought to himself, "This is just a game the Master is playing with me. He's testing me to see how determined I am. He's testing my commitment. I'll go at it one more time." Henry said, "Master, would you please check with God? How does God feel that I'm doing?"

The Master, after taking a very long deep breath, said, "Just a moment" and went into a trance. After a few minutes he opened his eyes. "What was your name again?"

"It's me, Henry!" he cried. Master nodded, "Ah yes. Give me a moment."

The Master, dramatically acting it out, waited for a while and then suddenly opened his eyes wide. He looked directly at Henry and said, "God does not know you exist."

Now Henry was at the point of tears as he walked out, utterly discouraged. Early the next morning, he packed up his belongings and left the Mystery School. He now works at an ashram where they do lots of ceremonies to connect with the Lemurians, the Pleiadians and the Ancient Ones, and perform many rituals to keep up with a long list of assorted makyo (also known as 'spiritual distraction').

That evening the Master was at the Embodied Masters Club when some of the other Masters said, "So, how did it go with Henry yesterday?" The Master replied with a touch of sadness, "Not well at all, at least not for now. Henry doesn't yet realize one of the most basic tenets of enlightenment: *When one does not recognize themselves, Spirit does not recognize them either.*"

\* \* \*

And that, dear friend, is the greatest gift of compassion that Spirit can offer.

When you do not recognize your own existence, when you rely on others for your measure, for your well-being, or to know whether you're doing it right or wrong; when you do not see yourself through your own eyes and hear yourself through your own ears; when you do not recognize yourself, Spirit doesn't recognize you either. Spirit doesn't know you exist until the moment *you* know you exist.

# Story 12

# In the Garden

*In honor of our families...*

The Master had a beautiful garden. He loved working in it because it taught him so much about the cycles of life. It taught him about birth as the plants and flowers burst into life each spring. It also taught him about death as the flowers and plants died at the end of each season, only to reawaken at the beginning of the next. The garden showed him that life continues.

One day, the Master was working in the garden as his dog, Hondo, played nearby. He loved Hondo because he understood that dogs are in such wonderful service. In a way, dogs are masters in their own right, not necessarily souled beings, but yet in service to humans. They're an extension of their Master, loving with such innocence and playfulness, and providing a true energetic support for the human.

On this day, the Master had an appointment with a student named Debra. She had called a few days earlier, urgently wanting to talk, so he had allowed time on this day to speak with her.

Debra arrived a few minutes early; she didn't want to miss the appointed time with the Master. She made her way to the garden and waited, feeling a bit annoyed that the Master continued working even though she was present. She had hoped he would sit down with her for a while so she could talk to him about her problems, but he kept on working, enjoying the feel of the earth and the plants, the warm sun, and the energy and essence of the garden. In fact, even though he knew it annoyed Debra, he still continued working. He knew this was for the best, because it would allow her to feel the energies of the ground and nature, and, perhaps, not be quite so caught up in her own dramas.

Eventually, the Master said, "So what is it, my dear student? What is it that you have come here for today?"

"Master," Debra replied, "I've been on this spiritual path for many years now, but I'm at the point of frustration. It feels like I'm going backwards instead of making progress. I'm literally at the point of letting go of my spiritual path, because I wonder sometimes if it's done more harm than good. I wonder if I'll *ever* be a Master, instead of always being the student. So, before I drop all this spiritual work, dump all the teachings and leave this group, I want to ask your advice."

The Master, still working in the dirt with his back to the student, answered, "Dear Debra, it is simply about letting go and Allowing." He knew this wasn't what she wanted to hear and, indeed, she retorted, "But Master, I *have* let go of nearly everything in my life!"

The Master paused for a moment, stood up to face her and said, "Yes Debra, you have let go of red meat and wine. You have let go of some of the religious groups you used to be involved in. But you still have not truly let go at the deepest levels. And without letting go, without releasing that old identity, it is very difficult to do this thing called Allowing. Allowing is where you release the things that are nearest and dearest in order for enlightenment to come to you.

"Remember, dear Debra, these cycles are natural. There is really nothing you have to do to bring them in. You've led yourself to believe that enlightenment is difficult and you have to struggle for it, but indeed it's not and you don't. Allowing is the deep, innate trust in yourself and in your own enlightenment, your own ascension, your own I Am. I see you letting go of little things on the surface and then thinking that you've let go of everything. Yes, perhaps you have let go of some of your personal possessions and old habits, but that's only part of Allowing. Without totally letting go, you're still connected to your identity and you'll continue to play the games you've always played."

The Master could see that Debra was not particularly happy about this message. She grumbled a little bit. She tried to take a deep breath, but could barely do it, so he continued. "Dear Debra, look at the situation. You still live within ten miles of the house that you grew up in as a child. You take care of your aging mother and father, and try to take care of your siblings in one way or another, even though you don't really get along with them. You have stayed in the same place for such a long, long time, but yet you tell me that you've let go??"

Debra considered his words for a moment. "But Master, I do this out of love for my parents. I watch over them and take care of their house. I stay close because I love them as they loved me when I was a child. To let go of them and move far away would be a disservice to them. It's not something I choose to do. Are you recommending that I just pack up and leave my aging parents to fend for themselves? That I neglect my family? That I turn my back on the love I have for them?"

The Master turned around and continued digging in the garden. He was actually smiling to himself, because he could have written the script of this whole conversation, for it wasn't the first time a student had approached him with the very same issues and problems. Finally, he said, "Dear Debra, it is up to you whether you want to move away and stop communicating with your family. In my own journey to become a Master, I felt it was necessary to move to a whole different country and not communicate with any of my family members for many, many years. It wasn't because I hated or even disliked them; it was that I needed the separation in order to come into my own.

"I learned later on that I actually didn't need to move at all, and neither do you. It is more about letting go of the energetic connections that you have with your family. You must realize that you have been on a long, long journey of ancestral karma that involves your biology, thoughts and actions. You have known these people in your family since long before you ever came to Earth, and you've spent many, many, many lifetimes with them. You're comfortable with them in many ways, even though there are also some things you resent.

"Ultimately, a Master realizes they do not belong to their family's lineage or biology. There comes a point when they have to acknowledge the souled being within each and every person, no longer seeing others as their mothers or fathers or brothers or sisters, but truly as unique souled beings. There comes a point when, in order to come into their own sovereignty, the Master no longer holds onto the connections of their family and ancestral past. But it is a very difficult thing for any soon-to-be Master to let go of those energetic connections, because they're so comfortable and familiar, and they have helped form your identity up to now."

The Master continued, "You don't need to move somewhere far away or stop caring for your parents. But you *do* need to change your perspective about who you are and who they are. You need to release the energetic ties, even within your body, so that your own light body can be incorporated into yourself, rather than living in your ancestral biology. You need to release the energetic connections that have kept you coming back into this same family for lifetime after lifetime after lifetime.

"As you release your family, you may find that it feels necessary to physically move away for a while, or perhaps not. But as you release them, you release a very, very strong part of your old identity. It is one of the most difficult and challenging things an initiate will ever do, but the blessing is that you *will* come into your own. You'll begin to understand your own true identity as a Master, and you'll begin to connect with and live out your own I Am. You'll adapt your own light body. You'll become yourself. And as you do, you're also going to release the family from this ancient bond that ties all of you together. You're going to give freedom to them as well as to yourself. Indeed, walking away from the family nest may be the greatest gift that you'll ever give to your parents."

Debra stared off in the distance, feeling almost stunned and imagining what it would be like to energetically release her family. Finally, after a few minutes of silence and contemplation, she said, "I hear your words, Master, but right now I feel it's very important to take care of my parents. Perhaps when they have passed on I can release them."

The Master smiled and thought to himself, "But even when the parents are gone, you'll hold their energy here. They'll still be part of your network, part of the bond that holds you together. You won't discover a *true* love with them, because you're simply loving them as your parents, almost as an obligation or debt." Out loud he simply said, "Dear Debra, the choice is yours. It is *always* yours. But do not come back to me until you have released your family, energetically and in every other way."

Then the Master turned around, called to his dog Hondo, and they walked off into the sunset beyond the garden. And Debra stood there with tears in her eyes.

* * *

Dear reader, I tell this story because you may still be very deeply connected to your family, whether it is your earthly biological or angelic family. For the one who truly desires to be an embodied Master on Earth, there comes a point where they must release the energetic bonds of their spiritual and biological family, and realize that these people are not truly their family. They are wonderful, beautiful souled beings, but they're not your family, just as your children aren't really your children. Perhaps they are dear friends, even kindred spirits, but you don't belong to each other.

It's about a total releasing so you can truly allow the enlightenment that is naturally yours. You'll face many, many things along the path that must be released so that the energy – and you – can be free. When you free the energies, you release yourself as well as the people who were involved in these things with you. You free yourself to be the I Am that I Am. You free yourself to go beyond the illusion of the identity you thought you were. It's been an interesting and sometimes beautiful identity, but it's not who you really are.

Debra had come to the Master hoping that he would tell her she needed something like a detox treatment or therapy or a certain book or some sort of exercise. She was greatly disappointed that the Master simply said, "It is time to release your family." She was feeling that she could no longer make progress on her spiritual path, but not really knowing what was keeping her back, thinking perhaps she just didn't have the right tools or enough intelligence. But she already had everything she needed. The fact is that she was so deeply enmeshed with her family and the family's history that she was not allowing herself to discover her own true identity.

She justified it by saying that she loved her parents, that she was close to her family and was taking care of them out of love and duty. But by focusing on her parents and siblings, she didn't have to take a look at herself. She tried to justify her existence by saying she was acting out of love, service and support to her family, but the Master knew it was all just a distraction.

Dear reader, whether you move to a different place or stay where you are, whether you change something in your life or not, if you are choosing to become an embodied Master it is time to release the *energetic* ties to your biological and spiritual families. You are at a point where these ties can serve as a convenient distraction to take you way from discovering and owning your passion, your truth, your true identity and your I Am.

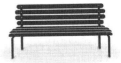

# Story 13

# The Musician

*Based on Master G...*

Back in the Mystery Schools of old, music was a very important part of both everyday life and the spiritual studies. Music was heard throughout the halls of the School during the day, and even gently into the night to lead the students off into the dream state on the harmonic notes. Music, such a beautiful human creation, is so very important in the sacred journey.

There is a type of music in the angelic realms, but it is not like the music here on Earth. Music on Earth is a vibration, an energy wave, floating through the air and meeting your ears, where it is translated by the mind into beautiful tones and rhythms. How could there be such fine music in the other realms where there is no physical reality to feel it or human ears to hear it? Indeed, music on Earth is such a special part of the spiritual journey and has always been important in the Mystery Schools.

As a matter of fact, we usually *sang* our words and greetings at the Mystery Schools, much like we did back in Atlantis, because it conveys more of the energy and feeling. Every student at the Mystery School played a musical instrument of some type so they could feel that vibration awaken something within their soul, and also bless and entertain others. In the Mystery Schools, we used music as a way of conveying sensory feelings and perceptions, so everyone would play. Sometimes it would be very harmonic and beautiful; other times it would be very dissonant, because that is music as well. It is much like human life. Sometimes, we would even transcend the music and go into silence, which of course is not really silent at all.

Indeed, there are those who seek silence, thinking everything will be quiet, but it's not. In the absence of external noise all the noise of the inner being can be heard, with its challenges and conflicts, as well as its beauty and harmonies. The silence is never silent as long as you are there, as long as consciousness is present.

\* \* \*

The Master was sitting in his room doing nothing, because that's what Masters do if they so choose – nothing. There was a knock at the door and he knew exactly what was coming next. The Master knew who was on the other side of the door and what the conversation would be; not every particular word, but certainly the beginning and the end of the conversation.

"Enter," he called out. The door opened and the student came in. The Master motioned for him to come sit near the warm fire and said, "Dear student, what is it on your mind?" The student was a very, very talented musician, and served as the Master of Music at this and several other Mystery Schools. But on this day he looked very troubled and frustrated.

The student settled into a chair, paused for a few moments and finally said, "Master, it's time." The Master nodded and the student continued, "We have gone beyond just words, from speaking to singing."

"Yes, yes. Nothing new," the Master said. The student continued, "And we do a lot of music that opens the soul, fills the heart and brings life to the dreams. It is true, real music." The Master said, "Yes, at times, it is."

The student paused again, then took a deep breath and came to his point. "I insist that, henceforth, at all of the Schools, there is no talking; that no words are used at all, not even singing. I insist that there be nothing but pure music. Look at the students. They're getting nowhere! They're learning very little. We need to go to the next step, and I insist that we take them there using only music and occasional times of silence."

The Master took a deep breath and, without using words to break the heavy silence, conveyed to the student exactly what he was thinking. But the student was so focused on in his agenda that he didn't feel what the Master was communicating.

Then the Master spoke aloud. "There are students who still feel the need and desire to speak, and they speak. There are those who still love the singing, and they sing. So, my dear friend, I don't think it's reasonable for you to ask that we only have instrumental music or silence. No, I don't think that's reasonable at all."

The student had anticipated this and was ready to put all his cards on the table. "Master," he said, "I love you dearly. We've been together for a long time. You have given me many opportunities and allowed me to share my passion for music with the students. But either we drop the words now, and use only music and silence to come into the pure and true mystical experience, or Master, I must leave."

Concealing a smile, the Master said, "Then so it is" and motioned to the door. The student was surprised. He thought there would be some negotiation, but he hadn't heard the silent words the Master had shared that said, "No negotiation, because then you end up with something less. You end up confused." The Master again motioned to the door and said, "Namaste."

The student grabbed his instruments and headed for the door, filled with anger and frustration. As he passed through the door, the Master said in very clear and audible words, "Don't let the door hit you on the way out."

And so it was that the Mystery Schools continued on with words, singing and music, and the silence that is never really silent.

\* \* \*

Approximately 473 years and many, many lifetimes later, the student was still playing his music. He had been doing it for lifetimes, traveling around the countryside, playing at small festivals and trying to teach humans the sacred mystical meaning of music. But not many listened. Not many understood the depths to which the student understood the sacred beauty of music.

Oh, and in those lifetimes, he often got frustrated with people. All they wanted was for him to play a cheerful little tune, something they could dance to, something they could use to escape from their dreary lives for a few moments. Although this annoyed the student, he played at some of these gigs anyway, believing it was the only way he could earn a living.

One day, he was playing at a Celtic Festival. Inside, he felt as if he was slowly suffocating, even dying, because they really didn't understand, and sometimes even thought to himself, "Maybe it really was better at the Mystery School. There they understood, at least to a degree, and certainly they understood better than these humans who just drink beer and scream at me to play more, faster and harder."

The student was living out yet another of these rather frustrating lifetimes that really didn't bring him any further along in his sacred music. Now he played simple bar music, good for drinking beer, but not much else. So it was that finally, in this lifetime, one day the student received a call out of the blue from someone who said, "Hey, I've got a gig for you. Do you want to play for this new spiritual group that's in town?"

Now, the student actually despised playing for most spiritual groups. He would almost rather play in bars and festivals than for a spiritual group, because at least the people accepted the music for what it was. At the spiritual gatherings, they pretended to know about sacred music. They pretended to understand and float off into the ethers, but the student knew in his heart that it was all just makyo; simply spiritual nonsense and distraction. So, when he got the call to play for this spiritual group he'd never heard of before, his first reaction was to say "No." But, well, he needed a few coins in his pocket, so he forced himself to accept.

He showed up at the appointed time and walked into the room with quite an attitude. He had a look of checking it out, because he was suspicious. Then he noticed that it didn't feel quite the same as a lot of other spiritual groups. There was something different about the people in the room, about what was going on. He shrugged it off and played the first set, as agreed, just before the main presenter came on. But he wasn't giving it his all or even putting his heart into it, because he really didn't care.

Then the presenter came on stage, and suddenly there was a transformation. Through the voice of what was just an ordinary human came the voice of the Master addressing the audience. And the Master commanded the student, "Come up here and play a new song. I want it to be called 'I Am that I Am' and we'll make it up as we go." The student felt a flash of anger surging through his body at being summoned up to the front and told to create a song in the moment without any preparation. He would much rather play at a bar or a festival than put up with this nonsense, but even so he came back up to the stage.

He felt something interesting and different about this Master, something he loved and something he also despised, because indeed he was meeting *the* Master once again. Yes, it was a different lifetime with a different body and a different name, and the Master was being channeled by someone else. But it was indeed the Master's energy.

So the new song was created. It was beautiful, and something happened in that moment. Something changed for both the student and the Master. The music woke up something within the student, an old passion, a remembrance of the Mystery Schools, and a fondness for this beautiful journey. He remembered a warmth and even a deep friendship with the Master. In fact, the impromptu song turned out so well that he and the Master continued to work together, traveling from land to land and gathering to gathering for many years.

Then one day they sat down and had a little chat. The student said, "I remember you. You were the Master of the Mystery Schools and now you're back. I remember the beautiful moments that we had, and I remember how I walked out, leaving behind so much that I loved."

The Master took a deep breath and said with a smile, "Ah, dear student, you were kicked out. It was time for you to go."

The student said, "Master, music is still such an important part of what we do, but I've learned a lot about it in these lifetimes on my own. I learned there's a lot more to it than just my own agenda. More than anything, I learned that there is something even beyond music."

"Oh, you are so right," the Master said. "Human words can help a person find their path because their ears hear and their mind understands. Whether they are words of spiritual teachers and philosophers, words of channelers, or words that are printed in books, the words help get one on a path, where before they might have had no idea that the path even existed. Then it is music that allows them to fly along the path, to rise up out of their purely human condition and soar like an angel along the path. And it is silence that allows them to go beyond, to transcend the path itself, to understand there is so much more beyond what is known.

"The words, the music and the silence are indeed very important. But, dear student, what I wanted to tell you, back on that fateful night at the Mystery School when I kicked you out, was that it's actually about wisdom. It is the wisdom that fills the cup of the soul. Not the words, not the music, not the silence, but the wisdom.

"When your soul first realizes 'I Exist,' you're like an empty chalice, a vessel waiting to be filled. Every experience a person has, every lifetime they live adds a few drops of wisdom to that chalice. No matter how much pain and suffering they endure, no matter how much anguish, no matter how many deaths they die, it all keeps adding wisdom to that cup. The soul begins to fill, feeling its existence in a way it never, ever felt before. It strips away all of the details like dates and times and even emotions, and distills everything right down to the core essence, the only thing that really matters, *the wisdom*.

"The soul keeps adding wisdom from every experience and every moment until it finally becomes so full of wisdom that it actually creates love. You see, love didn't come first. Wisdom came first, and it keeps filling and filling until at some point the soul overflows. And that, my friend, is called enlightenment. When that cup of the soul overflows with wisdom and falls back down upon itself, it is like you falling in love with yourself over and over and over again. You don't think about it. You don't try to create it. You don't tell yourself you love yourself. You just *do*. Imagine falling in love with yourself in every breath, in every action, in every moment, like a continual orgasm of love from soul back to soul.

"That, my dear old friend, is what fills the cup. Not words, not singing, not music and not silence. It's the wisdom."

The Master paused for a little while and they sat together in silence. Finally, he spoke again. "Dear student, I will never call you 'student' again. From now on I will call you Master G."

\* \* \*

This tale is based on a true story of one now known as Gerhard Fankhauser (oryom-music.com). About this story Adamus said:

*"We had some incredible encounters, heated debates, and many discussions of music. This one, Master G, had such a desire to work with every student at the Mystery School to bring them to a new level of consciousness through music, because it had brought enlightenment to him. Music helped him understand the sacred journey. But eventually, in this lifetime, he came to understand that it's wisdom that fills the cup of the soul.*

*"And now he plays beautiful music; music of the soul, music that makes the wisdom smile, music that shares a message, music that inspires. He still plays at a few bars and festivals, but now he's living in his passion."*

Gerhard and his music group Yoham play at many Crimson Circle events around the world. There is a unique and loving relationship between he and Adamus Saint-Germain. Together they created something called a "Merabh," which is a melding of Adamus' words and Gerhard's music. It provides a safe and musical space for the listener to allow an effortless and graceful shift of consciousness. On many occasions Adamus calls Gerhard up to the stage to create a new song in the moment, and each time the musical magic of Master G comes through.

# Story 14

# The Movie

*Inspired by a movie and several real people...*

The Master had asked Katarina to meet him at the movie theatre about twenty minutes before the movie started. Katarina was a new student. She hadn't been with the Master for very long and there were many things that she had not yet heard or experienced or applied in her life. Her energy was still somewhat chaotic and imbalanced, but she was a good student and tried very, very hard to follow her own heart. She tried to understand the wisdom the Master shared, but she was still in that in-between point of leaving her old human life and coming into her own Master's life.

The Master had seen it many times before; a new student with such desire and passion, wanting so much to realize their enlightenment, but yet with such a grip on their old lives. He had come to Katarina directly, because he could see that she was going through many difficulties and challenges. Even though enlightenment is supposed to be beautiful, she was very, very stressed and, like so many others, was going through tremendous difficulty on her way to Realization.

The Master sat down in the theatre at the appointed time with his box of buttered popcorn. Of course, as he already knew, Katarina was going to be late, because that's what happens to the humans who are going through this process into enlightenment but are still trying to deal with both worlds. She finally arrived, filled with apologies, making some panicked excuse about how she had gotten behind in her work, forgotten the time and missed the bus, and feeling very, very stressed out.

Katarina sat down next to the Master as he continued eating his popcorn and secretly smiling to himself, for he had seen this so many times before. Not the movie; the situation with Katarina. He finally said, "Katarina, what troubles you so much lately? Why have I seen so much stress with you?" Now she felt embarrassed and awkward, thinking that the Master could read her thoughts; that he could see into every part of her life. But her stress was so obvious that anyone could see it. The Master also knew that, in a time of change like she was in, the energies are high but also very imbalanced and chaotic.

Katarina answered, "I have so many problems and issues in my life right now and can't seem to make up my mind about anything." Gently, the Master said, "But specifically, what is it? What are these things in your life that are so difficult?"

Katarina took a deep breath and sighed, almost on the verge of tears. She wanted to be calmer in the presence of the Master, but she knew he could see right through that façade. It was obvious she was having difficulties. "Dear Master," she said, "The biggest problem is that I've been offered a job in another city almost 200 kilometers from here. It's a job I would probably like and the pay is higher than what I'm making now."

"But what is the problem with that?" the Master asked. "Well," she answered, "I've never lived so far away from my home town, and it would be very difficult and challenging to move to this other city. I would be away from my family and friends, and it would be quite an adjustment to sell my house and find a new place to live."

The Master looked at her kindly and said, "But truly, what is the real issue here?" Still very nervous and distraught, Katarina said, "I like my current job all right. It's not great, I don't have an important title, but the pay is adequate and it's very comfortable for me. On top of that, if I move to this new city, I couldn't participate in your schools and teachings. It has been my life's desire to explore, discover and pursue my spiritual Self. It's the most important thing in my life, and, with the new job, I would be far away, unable to have meetings with you or get together with the other students to share our thoughts and ideas. I would miss the friendship we all have together."

"And," she added, "It's a really big decision, moving away for this new job. How do I even know I'm going to like it? How long will I be there? How do I know it will be a good company to work for? I have a certain level of comfort now with where I live and what I do, but I'm so afraid to make a mistake or make the wrong choice or miss an opportunity."

Again the Master smiled to himself, knowing the dilemma Katarina was facing and aware that she was feeling a lot of anxiety about what to do. "Does it really matter?" he asked. "Of course it does!" she cried. "It's a huge life decision. What if I make the wrong choice? What if I take the wrong turn? What if it ends up being a disaster? I keep debating back and forth with myself about what to do. One moment, I feel it's best to stay with something I know and feel comfortable with; the next moment, I think I might like the bigger challenge. And, of course, having a better position and paycheck would certainly help. I'm absolutely torn between the two and just don't know what to do."

She paused for a moment and then continued, "Master, I have to tell you that I've called on the spirit guides and angelic councils. I've even called on you, dear Master, in the ethereal realms, to give me some guidance and help me know the answer."

"And have you received any guidance?" the Master asked. "I'm not sure," she replied. "One moment, I feel I may be getting an indication from some of the angels that I should do one thing or the other, and the next moment, I think I'm making it all up. I even went to some psychic readers, but the problem is that one reader said to take the new job and the other reader said not to take it. I've even tried using a pendulum, but the answer always comes back different. Now I'm totally confused. What are the energies trying to tell me? What is the universe trying to show me?"

The Master ate a little more of his buttered popcorn and looked at his watch to see how soon the movie would start, for he was very excited to see it. Then he said, "Katarina, it actually doesn't matter what you decide, because you cannot possibly get it wrong. Even if you *tried* to make a wrong choice, it would eventually correct itself. It really doesn't matter whether you take one job or the other, whether you move to a new city or not, whether you get a higher paycheck or not. There is truly no wrong choice.

"Humans get caught up in such drama! They make their choices into bigger affairs than they actually are. They will make a mountain out of a molehill, a little thing into a very big thing, and it's really not."

Now Katarina got a bit exasperated, feeling that the Master didn't truly understand her situation. Of course, he could feel her thoughts and said, "Well, *you* consider it a very, very big deal, but it's actually not. The important thing to realize is that, no matter what you choose right now, it will be the perfect choice. There's no right or wrong, no good or bad. Whatever choice you make will be absolutely perfect. And furthermore, no matter what you choose, all of the energies will continue to serve you. It's not about getting it right or wrong. It's simply about making a choice and keeping the energies moving.

"The universe is not trying to tell you anything by suddenly having the potential of a new job come up. The universe is not conspiring one way or the other, and it certainly has nothing to do with your astrological chart. It's not a test from the universe about whether you will make the right or wrong decision. It's simply there. And as soon as you begin to understand that, it will take away so much of the pressure, because you'll realize *it really doesn't matter*.

"You can take the new job and experience it for a short time or a long time. Either way, it's going to end up being the perfect thing. You can stay where you are and continue with the current job you have, and it will be the perfect thing. It's not that you're stuck or afraid to move somewhere else, because even if you decide to stay here, the energies will naturally continue to change and evolve to serve you.

"Dear Katarina, it's time to understand that everything that happens in your life – and I mean *everything* – is now about your enlightenment. Once a person makes a conscious and committed decision to awaken, to be the I Am Presence in their life; once they open the door to their own divine, it changes everything. It changes the entire way of life. Now *everything* that comes to you – every decision you make, every energy that opens to you, every opportunity that you seize or don't seize – it is *all* about your enlightenment. Therefore, you simply cannot make a bad choice. You *cannot* make a mistake.

"If you take the new job, the most appropriate situations will unfold for you. Whether finding a new house or making new friends, everything along the way will absolutely serve you. But the same will also be true if you don't take the new job. No matter what you choose, the energies will serve you. I know you're afraid that if you don't seize this new opportunity, it will mean that you're stuck or not moving forward and evolving. You think it's a sign from the universe that you're supposed to take the job in order to evolve, but it's not that way at all.

"You're going to evolve anyway, no matter what. You'll always have new energies and opportunities, new perspectives of life and new ways to experience the I Am in this beautiful human dimension. It's simply going to work out, no matter what you choose. Everything that happens to you is about your enlightenment, so please take the pressure off of yourself. Please stop thinking that this is some spiritual test where you have to make the right decision. It doesn't matter.

"I'm not just saying this metaphorically or as a nice universal expression; I mean it literally. *Everything* is about your enlightenment – every thought, every action, every experience. It's not the universe or the angels organizing to make it about your enlightenment; you are doing it for yourself at many, many different levels. Every part of you – your body, mind, spirit and consciousness – is aware that you are allowing yourself to receive the I Am, and therefore, everything that happens to you is absolutely in support of that.

"No other person, group or nonphysical being can interfere. They can be part of it. They can support your experience of coming into enlightenment, but they can't take it away from you. And you, my dear lady, cannot possibly make the wrong decision."

Katarina had been listening closely to every word the Master spoke. Some of it she still didn't quite believe, and some of it seemed more metaphorical than real. But as he spoke, she began to take his words in. Finally, breathing a deep sigh of relief, she realized how much pressure she had been putting on herself. Katarina realized that she had been looking at this as some sort of test, thinking there was a deep spiritual message she had yet to grasp. Now she began to realize the simplicity of the Master's words. It really *didn't* matter; it was simply about being in life and allowing herself to experience rather than trying to decide which experience would be better or worse than the other.

A tremendous sense of relief came over her entire being. The Master could see this, of course, and said, "Katarina, take a deep breath. Whether it is this issue of a new job or something simple like what to do on a Sunday morning; whatever issue or choice is in your life, *it doesn't matter*. You have transcended that whole dynamic of making right and wrong choices. Yes, other humans around you, especially those who are not yet awakening, are still in the consciousness of right and wrong, good and bad. They constantly have to measure themselves against their moral compass in order to decide if they're being good people or bad people. But once you make that deep and committed choice for enlightenment, it doesn't matter anymore. Then the only thing that matters is allowing yourself to enjoy the experience, to sense it at every different level and to be *in* life rather than fighting life; to *enjoy* life rather than being afraid of the choices that come along in life."

The Master paused and then said, "So, dear Katarina, now that you know it doesn't matter one way or the other, what will you do?"

Almost instantly, a new wave of panic and fear came over her. She wanted time to continue contemplating her decision, a little more time to think it over, but she also knew that would cause all the stress to come up again. Katarina took a deep breath, but this time it was nervous and awkward. The Master said, "It doesn't matter; just make a decision. Choose one or the other, but you must do it before the movie starts." He knew the movie would begin in about ninety seconds.

The panic and terror was even stronger now. Katarina hated the feeling that she might make the wrong decision. The Master watched her carefully and said, "Dear one, you now have less than thirty seconds to decide, because once the movie begins, I'm going to sit back and watch it."

Katarina took another deep breath and was instantly plunged into her deep, true feeling and knowing. She said, "I'm going to stay. I actually like my current job and I enjoy my life. I love the camaraderie with you and the other students. I'm going to stay."

Now the Master took a deep breath, feeling a great sense of relief for her. As the lights went down and the music started, the Master whispered to Katarina, "Now that you've made a choice, no matter what it was, the energies can start moving again. When you're in the consciousness of doubt, limitation and fear, the energies almost come to a standstill. But now you've taken tremendous pressure off of yourself and they can begin moving again. Now you can truly be in life again."

Katarina smiled and said, "Dear Master, I thought this job was a signal that I should be improving myself, that I should make more money and move to a different location. But I realize now that it was a false pressure, because I actually do enjoy my life. I don't need a better title, a better job or more money; I actually enjoy what I do."

As the music got louder and the opening titles scrolled across the screen, the Master said, "And the amazing thing is, Katarina, that it will only get better. What you like about life will only get richer, fuller and deeper. The universe is never trying to test you. It will never bring up opportunities to lure you into something else. The universe only desires your happiness. It was important for you to feel into the true choice, which was the knowing that you like what you're doing; therefore, there's no reason to do anything different. But watch now as the energies come in and make life even better, more rewarding, and more fulfilling for you."

They both took a deep breath and sat back to watch the movie. And, as the Master's eyes were fixed on the screen, Katarina reached into his bucket of popcorn and scooped out a big handful, a broad smile on her face.

\* \* \*

Dear friend, you often stress about choices in your life, but it really doesn't matter. There is not some sort of test from Spirit or the angelic councils or even from me. There are, indeed, opportunities that come up, but it doesn't mean that you need to take them. They are simply choices to consider and it doesn't matter which one you make. You put tremendous pressures on yourself until you're almost immobilized and unable to make *any* decision, but this isn't a spiritual test to see how smart you are or which decision you can get correct. Things will always come up in life, and as long as you live in human form, there will always be decisions to make and things to do.

I ask you now to make your choices with the understanding that you cannot get it wrong. And if for some reason you make a choice that is not congruent or resonant with your embodied enlightenment, it will self-adjust; not through Spirit or anyone else, but from within you. You have an internal automatic guidance system called the I Am, and it will set you on the course that is absolutely perfect for you, regardless of which direction you choose in any moment.

Feel into what you would really like to do, without all the mental confusion that comes with doubt and uncertainty. Choose what you like best without getting all caught in the energies and conflicts. Choose what makes your heart sing. And understand that, no matter what choice you make, it will lead to your embodied enlightenment.

# Story 15

# Too Much Noise

*Based on an actual encounter with the Master...*

The student's alarm clock woke her up before the sun and she yawned, wondering why Masters schedule their meetings with students so early in the morning. She wasn't used to getting up at this hour, but on this particular day she had to, for she had requested a meeting with the Master.

Getting dressed she felt anxious. Nobody really likes approaching the Master with deeply personal questions and it was well known that the answers are not usually what one expects or wants. But things in her life had been in such turmoil that she had requested this urgent meeting, and it had been granted for five o'clock in the morning.

As the student made her way to the Master's big, beautiful home, she wondered what it would take for her to someday have a home of this magnitude and grandeur. Feeling butterflies in her stomach as she approached the door, it opened by itself. She knew she had to find her way to the Master within his very large house and, moving tentatively through the halls, every step seemed like torture. At last, she found him out in the garden, enjoying his coffee and a fresh French croissant, watching the sun come up. As he listened to the birds singing and watched the Earth come to life on this new day, a smile filled his face.

The student approached him slowly, "Master, I'm so sorry to trouble you, but I'm at my wits end." "Never apologize," the Master said.

Feeling she had already gotten off to a bad start by making the wrong statement, she took a deep breath and started again. "Master, my life is in total chaos and confusion. I can't seem to collect my thoughts anymore, my body aches, my stomach is constantly churning and my joints are in so much pain that I can barely get through the day. I just don't know what to do anymore, so I've asked for this meeting with you. What can I do?" The Master took another slow, deliberate sip of his coffee, almost as if he didn't even hear her words. Finally, he said, "Dear Sally, it's not yours." Sally said, "But Master, you don't understand. I am in pain, emotionally and physically. I can barely keep myself together. I need *something*, whether it's a blessing or some sort of transformation or some kind of healing. I need *something* because it's all falling apart." "So, what is going on in your life?" the Master asked. "What's all this chaos?" "Oh," she cried out, "My children! They don't call anymore, and when they do, it's always to start an argument or ask for something. There's just no compatibility between us, no close relationship like I always hoped to have with them."

The Master, with something close to a grin on his face, said, "But it's not yours. Neither are your children. What else, dear Sally? What else?" "Master, the world is falling apart too! When I watch the news or read the newspapers, when I talk to other people, everyone can see that everything is falling apart. The crazy weather, the wars, the crime, the poverty and problems all over the world – it's just too much for me to handle." And the Master, sipping on his steaming cup of coffee, said, "But it's not yours."

Now Sally was getting frustrated. "But Master, these things *are* affecting me. I feel like my life is falling apart, like I have no connection with myself. I hear strange voices in my head all the time and can't seem to turn them off. Please, what can I do? Isn't there any sort of healing that we can do here?" The Master, again very patiently, said, "All of these thoughts, all of these things going through your head, they are not yours."

Sally was beginning to get angry. She could feel the anxiety mounting and it was affecting her body and mind. She couldn't even think of the next appropriate question to ask the Master and, for a long time, she just stood there wondering what to do. Finally, she asked, "But Master, then what *is* mine? You say these issues with my children, my financial challenges, the bad news in the world and all of these things aren't happening, but they are! They're affecting me. They're affecting my physical and mental well-being. If these things aren't mine, then what *is* mine?"

The Master sat very patiently, truly understanding her angst, and said, "That is for you to answer, not me. Only you can discover what is truly yours. Now, dear Sally, it's time for you to leave so that I can enjoy my morning breakfast, and please don't come back until you can answer this question: What is yours?"

\* \* \*

Dear reader, there is tremendous energy noise everywhere, at a level unprecedented in modern history. There is noise coming from everything, and you're dealing with it each and every day from the moment you wake up in the morning.

Some of the energy noise comes from Earth itself, from nature and trees, and that noise is generally in resonance with you. But there are many other energies that are out of resonance, especially as you allow your enlightenment and become more sensitive, and you're going to feel these things more than ever.

For instance, you're going to feel traffic. Yes, it makes a physical noise with the rumbling of engines and tires on the road, but you're also feeling the tension of the people driving down the highway. There is tension in a traffic jam with the issue of safety and getting to work on time. And usually, when people are sitting in a traffic jam or waiting at traffic signals, they are thinking more than ever, and the thoughts aren't generally peaceful, abundant and joyful. The thoughts are about things they haven't taken care of, projects they have to complete, emotional relationships with others. When you put this all into a traffic jam, can you imagine the noise? Indeed, you can, because you put up with it every day.

Then, you get to work in your office and there is noise from your co-workers and all the office equipment, even from the wireless networks. There are more machines than ever before and they are all emitting noise, even if you don't hear it with your ears. There's energy noise in food and in the air around you, particularly if it is polluted. There is energy noise coming from the people around you. There are more humans on Earth right now than ever before in the history of this planet, which means there is more congestion, more human and mental noise everywhere.

Energy noise begets more energy noise. In other words, if you are surrounded and overwhelmed by energy noise from machines, electronic signals, other people, nature and all these other things, then you get more tense, and it's more difficult to determine what is yours and what's coming from the outside. So, what do people do to overcome the noise? They put on headsets, listen to music, and play even more noise on top of the noise, which, of course, begets even more noise. You end up with a very, very noisy reality to the point where, like Sally, you can't discern anymore what's yours and what is coming from the outside. It enters into the body and you start feeling it in your shoulders, back, belly and heart, and soon you can't hear your own thoughts or your own true feelings.

It used to be that when humans would go to sleep at night, they would transcend the noise level. They would go into a dream state far beyond the noise and get true rest. But now, those dream states are permeated by the very noise that you're trying to get away from. Even while you're sleeping, it's noisy, sometimes even noisier than when you're wide awake. Noise is everywhere. And, because of hypnotic programming and conditioning, and simply because of the fact that you're constantly in the midst of noise, you forget what's yours and what's not. You start to absorb it all, and then you do all sorts of strange things to try to handle and manage all this noise, rather than saying to yourself, "This isn't mine."

It doesn't mean that you have to desensitize yourself or put a shield or barrier of white light around yourself, because that's unnatural. You only have to remember what is yours and what is not.

Take time by yourself in nature. Spend time with people who have an energetic resonance with you, those who are kindred spirits. Then choose what's yours and what's not. You'll be surprised to discover that over 95% of the thoughts going through your mind and the feelings in your body are actually not yours. Then you can simply choose what you *want* and let the rest of the noise fade away.

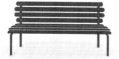

# Story 16

# The Dolphin

*Inspired by someone with a lot of problems...*

The Master was sitting under an umbrella, enjoying the peaceful and refreshing atmosphere at the beach. On this beautiful sunny afternoon, he was whittling a piece of driftwood, carving the likeness of a dolphin. The Master loved carving and he spent many joyful hours creating beautiful little sculptures. Sooner or later, he always ended up giving them to one of his students as a reminder of some particular lesson they were experiencing.

So it wasn't a surprise, sitting in his comfortable chair with a Mai Tai and the little dolphin, that he saw Stella, one of his students, coming down the beach. She was walking very fast and almost didn't notice the Master, simply nodding toward him as she passed by in a rush. The Master stopped carving and said, "Stella! Stop for a moment. Come have a seat and let's chat." Flustered, she paused and looked at the Master. But, being in such a dither, she just couldn't bring herself to come sit down.

The Master said, "Where are you going in such a hurry?" She answered, "Master, can't you see the clouds over there? A storm is coming!" The Master noticed the storm clouds were at least 30 kilometers away; he wasn't worried. Then Stella added, "Besides, I have to get ready for dinner." Glancing at his watch, the Master said, "But Stella, it's only four o'clock. Dinner's not till 6:30 tonight. Why the hurry?"

"Master," Stella said, becoming annoyed at his questions, "I have a lot to do to get ready for dinner and I don't want to get caught in the storm. As a matter of fact, you should fold up your chair and go inside as well. That storm might get really bad."

The Master smiled and said, "Stella, stop and take a deep breath for a moment. That storm is a long way off, and I really don't think it will get here any time soon. In fact, I think it will go the other way and won't even get here at all. And Stella," he added, "The sun is shining, the air is calm, and you have two and a half hours before dinner. Stop, relax, have a Mai Tai. Ease up for a bit." Stella was fidgeting and he already knew that she couldn't accept his invitation. It was her nature to worry about everything.

"Stella," he said. "I've been watching you, I notice things. And I can see that, even though you study and work hard at all this spiritual stuff, you're always stressing, always worried about something. What's that about?" Stella still felt anxious and wanted to get on her way, but she also didn't want to be rude to the Master. "Well, Master," she answered, "There's always something to worry about. If I don't handle things or manage everything properly, it could all fall apart. If I don't go inside, I might get caught in the storm and get sick. If I don't get ready for dinner, something might happen to make me late. And then I won't get a good seat."

The Master replied, "Stella, you worry about everything! You even worry about cancer." Stella was a little taken aback, for she hadn't talked about this to anyone. "But cancer runs in my family, which means there's a very good chance I'm going to get it too."

"Stella," the Master said, "You worry about money." Now she was really annoyed, "That's because I never have any! I'm constantly trying to figure out how I'm going to pay the rent, how I'm going to pay for this stupid school, for my meals, everything. Of course I worry about money. I *have* to!"

The Master continued, "You're always worried about your thinking, always trying to manage the thoughts in your mind." Stella answered, "Yes, of course I try to manage my thoughts! Otherwise, I get so many negative thoughts coming in and then negative things start happening. So, yes, I have to at least try to control my mind and thoughts."

The Master took a deep breath. "Stella," he said, "You worry about so many things that aren't very likely to happen; in fact, they probably *won't* happen. I think you actually like worrying. It's become your way of life and you just don't know anything else."

Stella really didn't like this last comment. She was used to people saying things like, "Oh, you poor dear. You've had such a bad life, things are so tough for you," and now the Master was saying that she actually *liked* all this worrying. It didn't even make sense. She had already lost too much time with this ridiculous conversation and was ready to turn away when the Master said, "Stella, it's a type of compulsive addiction to always worry about what isn't actually there. It's really a waste of time and, more than anything, it keeps you stuck in your thoughts, always thinking and worrying about everything, because you think you have to. You think that's how you manage to hold everything together."

By now, Stella was getting quite angry with the Master for speaking to her like this. The Master could see that she was tightening up and said, "Stella, you are in your thoughts all the time. Even though we, in this school, are constantly talking about consciousness, you're always in your head. Thoughts can be very fearful and they can make you neurotic, like you are sometimes." She frowned, but the Master continued.

"Stella, here's the difference between thoughts and consciousness. Thoughts will put you on a very linear path and have you worrying about everything. They will have you worried about cancer, about money, about being late to dinner – about everything – and this greatly limits your reality. But consciousness, awareness, is totally different. For example, I don't worry about that storm over there, because I'm in awareness, which is very different than thought. Being in awareness means I'm not thinking about the next storm that might come up, not at all. It may or it may not. I may get rained on, but I probably won't.

It's not because I'm forcing the clouds to go off another way, but because I'm simply in awareness, rather than thought, so I don't worry about it. You, Stella, are thinking all the time. And all that energy behind the thinking will cause you to get caught in a lot more storms than you ever need to."

Stella was listening now, in spite of her anxiety, and the Master continued, "I'm in awareness, and right now the awareness is that there's a storm; it may or may not affect me. The awareness is not worrying about it, but rather understanding that I am always absolutely in the right place, *no matter what happens*. And that, Stella, is the difference. You worry that it is going to happen because of your thoughts. I am in total awareness, not at all worried about what might happen, and then it usually doesn't. By the very fact of trying to control your thoughts, you are actually bringing in the very energies that cause a lot of conflict, stress and storms in your life. I'm simply not in that.

"You think, Stella, that my life is good because I'm the Master. You think I'm supposed to be holy and that I'm powerful enough to push storms away; that I work at having abundance and make sure I have thoughts that avoid cancer, but this is not true at all. I don't need to do any of that. I don't need to think about avoiding cancer, having abundance, moving storms or anything else. I am in awareness. I Am that I Am. I Exist. I am here right now, in a wide variety of potentials, but I'm not thinking about them. And somehow, everything just seems to work out."

The Master paused for a moment, watching Stella's reaction. He could see that part of her was beginning to understand that maybe she really could just live and be free. He continued, "You know, Stella, we have a sign in the Ascended Masters Club. It hangs above the door to the Comedy Room. And yes, we have a Comedy Room, because every Ascended Master has walked as a human before, gone through the very things that you're going through now, and has gotten over them. Then we go tell stories in the Comedy Room about our neuroses, fears and limitations, and they are truly funny. Anyway," the Master said, "There's a beautiful sign above the door that simply says: 'It all works out.'

"You see, Stella, it all works out, and that's the joke. The human worries about all these different things, because they're out of awareness, out of consciousness, and into their thoughts. They forget that it all works out, and not just for the Ascended Masters; sooner or later, it works out for everyone, if they allow it. I know that's hard for a human to do, because they feel assaulted by a lot of things, such as the fact that they might get cancer or might go broke. But if you're in awareness; if you're in consciousness in the moment, those things probably are not going to happen.

"It all works out. As a matter of fact, it *has* already worked out, because time and space are an illusion. There's no past and future. There is you in the Comedy Room at the Ascended Masters Club, telling jokes about when you worried about things like storms that never show up, being late for dinner, and getting a disease. It has already worked out. You're already there."

The Master paused and took a deep breath. "Could you just be with that, Stella? Could you put down the worrying? Could you step out of that pattern? Could you stop attracting those energies into your life? I know it's a very bold step, but could you just allow yourself to know that everything has already worked out?"

Stella, having forgotten all about the storm, contemplated the Master's question. Suddenly, she took a deep breath and said, "I'll think about it, Master. But right now, I've got to get ready for dinner."

"But before you go," the Master said, "Let me give you this little carving that I made. Notice that the dolphin has a bit of a smile on its face; that's because it's free. The dolphin just swims in the ocean, not worrying about where the next meal will come from, not worrying about dying or getting lost. It just swims in the ocean, plays with the other dolphins and enjoys the moment. Stella, at one point, you were that dolphin, and I mean that literally. A long time ago, when you first came to Earth, you were a dolphin, simply glad to be in the experience of life and biology. I'm giving you the gift of this little carved dolphin to remind you of who you really are: a free being in experience."

Stella thanked the Master and rushed off, relieved to finally be able to get ready for dinner.

\* \* \*

Dear friend, it all works out. Just know that. Why have all the stress? Why worry about storms that will probably never come? Why have all the worry about abundance, which really puts you in lack? Why worry about diseases that will likely never manifest?

Sometimes, humans put themselves through strange experiences such as getting cancer, but why? The reason is because, through that experience, they learn about the beauty of life. When life is being taken away, they can finally experience its beauty. But you don't have to do it that way. You don't have to set up those harsh and difficult experiences in your life. You don't need to have lack in order to understand abundance. Those days are gone.

It is truly a breakthrough when a human can go from their thinking mentality into simple awareness. Like the Master told Stella, thinking about everything just limits potentials and energies. The Master is in awareness, rather than thinking, and there's a huge difference.

In awareness, you're not worried about the storm; in thinking, you're worried "Is the storm coming this way? Is it going to flood my house? Will I get hit by lightning?" The energies are so very different. The Master in awareness notices the storm and keeps whittling, making little dolphins for the students.

In awareness, the thoughts may still be there, for that's the "and." But when you come to awareness – "I Am that I Am, I Exist; now I'm going to have fun" – it changes all of the patterns and dynamics; it changes the energy that comes to you. In awareness, you're ready to bring in more energy without worry of burning out your body or mind. There's no need to filter or limit anymore; you're ready for it, and the energies realign and shift to facilitate that.

It all works out. It's effortless. No work or thinking required. It's all about Allowing.

The Master, whittling away on the beach, is not worried about storms or dinnertime or even how his school is going, for there is no need. Why worry and stress? Simply let the energies come in as they respond to consciousness. Instead of having to manage and worry about everything, the Master Allows. Therefore, the energies are naturally in alignment, coming in to serve the Master according to the awareness.

Dear friend, let energy come to you, into your life – soft, beautiful energy – without force. It doesn't even have a positive or negative charge; it is just energy coming in, filling your body and mind, coming into all of your life. Let there be nothing holding it back anymore, like Stella with all of her fears. Let there be no resistance; no ifs, ands or buts; no wondering if you're worthy. Of course you're worthy! Let there be no worrying that you might do something bad with it, no worrying that you're depriving someone else; there's plenty of energy for everyone. Just take a deep breath and Allow as it comes to you.

Don't even worry about what you're going to do with all this energy. You're just going to swim in it, dance with it, feel it, experience it. The Master Allows the energies to come in, without worrying about what to do next, because it all works out. This is freedom, by the way. Freedom is letting energy come into your life and serve you; not by demand or manipulation or force, but by Allowing.

The Master was trying to help Stella understand that when you're constantly thinking and worried about everything, you are drastically limiting the energy that is available to you. It's there, but you're simply not aware of it. When you're constantly thinking about problems and what's coming next and lack of abundance and what you should be doing in life, then you're not aware of the energies that are already there. It is self-limiting. As the Master said to Stella, you can let all that go. Be aware, be the "I Exist," and then have fun. And suddenly, you'll realize how much energy is there for you; how much was *always* there. It's yours, without work, without effort or focused thoughts or meditation or anything else like that. You just Allow it and receive it. The sign at the Ascended Masters Comedy Club, "It all works out," imagine that within yourself. It all works out, because you're allowing it to.

\* \* \*

Stella was pretty irritated with the Master for a while; so irritated, in fact, that she went out of her way to worry even more, just to prove it was what she needed to do. She told herself that the Master was just some crazy old coot who didn't understand her problems, and that all he had were these overused phrases and clichés. But, after a couple weeks, she thought, "I'm tired of running from storms. I'm tired of always being worried about the next disease or physical problem. I'm so tired of constantly worrying about everything." She finally admitted to herself that she *was* caught up in the game. It *was* sort of an addiction, always being worried. And, more than an addiction, it was an excuse for not really being in life. It helped that, every day, she saw the little wooden dolphin on her nightstand, for it reminded her to live free; that this is just an experience and it all works out.

One day, she finally she got up the courage – or maybe it was the lack of pride – to go talk to the Master again. "Master," she said, "You're right. All my life, I've been so preoccupied with worrying and stress. It's even why I came to this school, but it was just another way to focus on the stress, because I tried to apply all the spiritual principles to the fear and stress and worry. But I finally realized I've been cutting off the flow of energy. I was just not living. Master, I don't care what it will take, but I'm going to let all that go. Actually, I really don't have that many problems, and the ones I do have are about other people. I am ready to go beyond all that and be an energy designer. I'm ready to live."

The Master smiled and said, "It's going to feel a little strange now. Every time your mind pops back to problems and worries, it will be a little strange at first to just take a deep breath and be in awareness rather than in fear. It will take some courage to trust that it all works out." Stella answered, "That still sounds better than the flat gray life I've been living, full of fear and doubt and lack. Master, from now on, when the fear comes up, I'm going to take a deep breath and remember that it all works out."

# The End of the Path

*Inspired by countless spiritual seekers...*

The Master sat high on the branch of a tree, disguised as a large black crow. Masters can do this, of course. It doesn't actually mean that they take on the biological body of an animal; it means they can shape-shift their energy to give the illusion to the observing human that they're something other than who they truly are. Actually, the true Master understands that it's *all* an illusion, whether they appear as a human, as a Master dressed in their Master robes or as a large black crow sitting on the branch of a dead tree. The Master can be anything they wish and many things simultaneously.

The Master sat watching from the old tree as the student approached, walking along the path. Her name was Margo and she was very earnest and committed in her spiritual journey, perhaps because her life had been so miserable. It had been filled with abuse from and toward other people; filled with days and nights of too much drinking, which ultimately turned her into an alcoholic; filled with the shame of abandoning her own children. It was a life so wretched that she finally felt there was almost no choice other than this spiritual path.

Margo had worked hard, studied hard, and had actually been one of the Master's very best students. But now came the moment of reckoning. She was coming to a place on the path that had stopped many others before her. Walking slowly along, she came to a sign and stopped. As she looked down and saw the skulls and bones of others who had died when they had gotten to this point, she knew it was more than just a wooden sign; it was an important message, a point of separation. She also realized that she could not see up ahead beyond the sign, for there was nothing but a thick mist or fog that completely obscured the path. She knew this was meaningful as well.

Margo read the message on the sign and took a deep breath, wondering what it meant for her. The sign had one simple word on it: "Forgive." That was all. This brought up a tremendous amount of emotion and sadness in Margo, for she knew she had hurt many, many others in her life. She took another deep breath and felt into what this word "forgive" meant to her, and knew she had to turn back. She could go no further until she had received the forgiveness of everyone she had ever hurt, and there were many.

With a heavy heart Margo turned around and went back to her town, back to all the people with whom she'd ever had, let's say, an energetically imbalanced relationship. For the next three and a half years, she knocked on doors, made telephone calls and had many tearful meetings with those whom she had harmed, asking forgiveness for what she had done to them. Most were a bit shocked and confused when she first approached them. Some even asked, "What do you want me to forgive you for?" and then she would have to bring up all those dark, buried and very fearful memories of what she had done.

Most people were willing to forgive her without thinking twice about it. Some even felt that her request for forgiveness meant they had finally won. And yes, for some there was also a bit of energy feeding and power playing going on.

A few people found it very, very difficult to forgive Margo. One of these was her daughter, who, because of having a mother who was constantly drunk, had gone through so many difficulties, crises and challenges of her own. The daughter felt lonely and abandoned, for indeed she *had* been abandoned, and it was several years before she was actually able to forgive her mother. Even then, it wasn't a true forgiveness. It was more pity and shame for the mother, rather than a true release of the energies.

Another who found it difficult to forgive Margo was one of her ex-husbands. He had actually been very, very abusive with her and had used her for his own purposes and energy feeding. He found it difficult to forgive, because his energy hooks were still embedded into her. He was still feeding off of her, still manipulating her through their children, but eventually, even he forgave her and basically let her go.

Finally, after three and a half years of begging for forgiveness, Margo got back on the spiritual path again. She returned to the very place where her journey had previously stopped and, once again, she saw the sign that simply said, "Forgive." The Master was there too, once again disguised as a black crow sitting on the branch of the old dead tree. As Margo looked at the sign and wondered if she had truly gotten the forgiveness that she had asked for, the crow let out a very loud cry.

Margo looked ahead and saw that the path was still obscured with fog so thick it was impossible to tell what lay ahead. Was it a chasm? A stone wall? What was next?

She sat down at the foot of the sign and asked within herself for an answer. "What am I supposed to do? Have I truly, truly received forgiveness for all I have done against others?" Margo sat there beneath the sign for two full days without eating, drinking or even sleeping, trying to understand why the fog was still there and why she felt a deep unsettled feeling about this whole issue of forgiveness.

When she was nearly delusional from not eating or sleeping, the answer suddenly came to her. You know what that's like; the answers often come when you're tired, disoriented, maybe even delusional, because they can finally get through the thick mental veil. When that veil is weakened, the answers can sometimes come in so strong and clear that there's no doubt. You may doubt later on, but in that moment you absolutely know.

What Margo realized in that moment was that the word "Forgive" on the sign was not about seeking the forgiveness of others. It was about Margo forgiving herself, and *that* was a very difficult truth for her to realize. In a way, it had been easy for her to go back for three and a half years and revisit all of those with whom she had had relationships. That was easy in comparison to forgiving herself.

Once again, the large black crow high up in a tree screeched out, confirming that she was absolutely correct. It was about forgiveness of herself.

Metaphorically speaking, Margo is still sitting under that sign wondering, "How do I forgive? What do I forgive?"

* * *

Dear reader, this is your story. You've cleaned up so many things in your life. You've gone back emotionally and sometimes literally to make amends and to release. You've gotten this far on the path, and now the Master cries out and says, "It's time to forgive *yourself.*"

To this day, Margo still hasn't moved forward. To her, the path is still shrouded mist, because she feels the confusion of not knowing what lies beyond forgiveness. But I am happy to share with you what's there, just beyond the sign. It is the threshold, the final step into embodied enlightenment, and it's not at all what you suppose it to be.

What's ahead is the doorway, the crossing point. But before you step through it, there must be total and unconditional forgiveness. I call it unforgiving forgiveness or unrelenting forgiveness, for there is no partial or incomplete forgiveness from here on. There is no "kind of" or "sort of" forgiveness. It's all or nothing.

Unforgiving forgiveness means that nothing about yourself is left untouched. The skulls and bones Margo had noticed beneath the sign were remnants of the ones who could not move forward; who were baffled by the whole concept of true forgiveness. It's not about others forgiving you; that has little or no meaning. It's not about you forgiving others, whether your parents or your inner child, bad teachers, bad partners or anyone else. Forgiving others is meaningless when you come to this point. It is about the unforgiving, unrelenting forgiveness of *yourself.*

Perhaps you feel you've already done that. Perhaps you feel you've learned to love yourself and have gotten over the issues with yourself. I would reply that you've seen only a few of what could be hundreds or thousands of layers. You've learned to adapt and adjust in order to survive. You've learned to forgive enough so you didn't absolutely torment yourself. But, dear friend, there is so much that lies beneath, still unforgiven.

You continue to accumulate guilt on a daily basis, even if you're not consciously aware of doing so. It's there in the form of judgments, limitations and holding back. It's there in the ways you deal with yourself energetically; in other words, the energies that you allow into your body and into your life. It's there in the way you shine your light around other people and the ways you try to conform or be normal or fit in.

Dear friend, the unforgiving forgiveness does not allow that anymore. There is no more hiding, no more holding back, no more depriving yourself of anything. At this point on the path, when you see the sign that says, "Forgive," understand that it goes far beyond this thing called love, even love for yourself. Love is such a beautiful human thing, but, spiritually speaking, it is far 'below' forgiveness. In other words, far more than simply loving yourself, crossing that threshold is about the unforgiving forgiveness.

Fortunately, this forgiveness is not something you have to work through step by step, point by point, issue by issue. In fact, it's quite the opposite, for once you step through that door, it will come over every part of you in the most unrelenting and complete way you could possibly imagine. Remember also that this unrelenting, almost brutal forgiveness is there in the greatest love, compassion and service to you. It's not there to punish you for things done wrong, but rather to clear, to cleanse and to move. But there will be times when you feel it's the worst storm you've ever gone through.

My advice is to let go. Don't try to control or manipulate, and don't resist. Understand that this unforgiving forgiveness is going to come into every part of you, and not just the version of you that sits here reading this book. It will come into every past life and every potential future experience. It will be an incredible, overwhelming, sometimes painful but beautiful cleansing.

# Story 18

# The Temple

*Based on a true story of an Ascended Master...*

It was late in the night when the student heard a knock at the door. It woke her up from a deep, sound sleep, and, for a moment, she hoped it was only a dream. But the knock persisted. A feeling of dread came over the student, for she knew this was the moment she had both anticipated and feared. She delayed getting out of bed, hoping that perhaps the knock was on someone else's door. But no, it was hers.

She took a deep breath and felt a cold emptiness in every part of her body as she slowly got out of bed. Reaching for her shawl and putting on her shoes, the knock persisted and she knew now that it was indeed for her. There was no question about it and there would be no delay. She blew out the candle in her room, quietly made her way down the stairs and went out into the cool night air. For a moment, she thought about bolting, running away right now, but something kept her on the path that led toward the temple doors.

It was the night of the full moon, and all was quiet and still. Hardly a sound could be heard, save the hooting of an owl in the distance. She made her way across the empty courtyard, peering at her destination in the distance. She could barely breathe now, thinking about that knock at the door and what it meant.

Finally, after what seemed like hours (but was actually only a few minutes), she approached the large wooden doors of the enormous temple. She had never seen these doors open before, nor had she ever seen anyone actually go into the temple, but she knew this is where it happened. This was the moment of truth. They hadn't given her any instructions, but it was known here in the Mystery School that when you had the knock at the door, it was your time to go to the temple.

Now she wondered why they had never given any instructions. Certainly this was some type of important ceremony, the closing of many, many old chapters, if not the entire book of her life. All her years of studying, all the heartaches and tears, all the struggles would come to a point right here and now. Her mind was filled with doubt. Her palms got sweaty and her breath was short as the student wondered what she should do next. In her anxiety, she forgot nearly everything she had learned over the years in the Mystery School, things like knowingness and synchronicity and Allowing, and she just stood there trembling.

Suddenly, the great doors of the temple slowly swung open by themselves, as if by magic. She peered inside and didn't see anybody or anything that could have possibly opened them. It was all very mysterious, intriguing and quite frightening, but she knew it was time for her to cross the threshold and go inside. She knew this was it.

The student had been in the Mystery School for a long, long time. Some twenty years prior, she had felt the urge and heard the inner call to come to the Mystery School, and she had abandoned her children and her loving and wealthy husband in order to go. In the School, she had learned so much about life, about herself, about her journey and about the true meaning of love. And now, with the doors of the temple wide open, even though no one was there to greet her, she knew it was time. There would be no ceremonies or processions, just her, the temple door and the hooting owl.

She took a deep breath, knowing it was time to enter, but that first step was difficult. Her feet felt heavy, as if they were cast in concrete. She could barely lift them, barely summon the courage to step inside, and once again she wondered why there had been no instructions or information about what to expect or what to do. She finally took that first step and entered the temple. As her eyes adjusted to the darkness, she realized the temple was huge. It was much larger inside than it appeared to be from the outside, and she wondered how this could be. How it could look one size on the outside and three or four times bigger on the inside?

As she stood wondering about this, the doors closed by themselves with a thud. Now there was no turning back, no running out. Now it was just her, the temple and the Master.

The student took a deep breath and tried to get her bearings. Now that her eyes were a bit more adjusted to the darkness, she could make out a human figure at the far, far end of the temple, illuminated only by dim candlelight. She knew it was the Master, and it was her time to approach.

The stone floor of the temple was ancient but clean. The ceiling was huge and vaulted, disappearing into the darkness. She took the first step on the cold, hard floor of the temple and wondered, "How many others have come before me? How many others have stood here, filled with dread and terror, not knowing what to do? How many others?" Slowly, she took another step and another, so very slowly, hearing her footsteps echo on the walls of the temple. It was so large and empty that every little sound seemed magnified as it echoed throughout the chamber.

Feeling more terrified with every step, she slowly continued, moved along by something within. It was her knowingness that came forth, compelling her to take one step and then another, slowly, slowly moving toward the Master. "No rushing," it told her. "No pushing. Savor every moment." But her body wasn't responding how she wanted it to. Her knees were trembling and she felt as if she would collapse at any moment. Wishing she had used the toilet before coming to the temple, the student stopped for a moment, took another deep breath to steady herself, and continued the slow journey.

Then she began to despair. "Why do they make this so long?" she thought. "Why couldn't they just have the Master meet me right inside the door? What is the purpose of this endless walk?" Then, in a moment of terror, she thought, "Perhaps this is a test. Perhaps I'm supposed to do something or say something here." She got very confused, wanting so much to do the right thing that she broke out in a cold sweat. She had been working toward her Realization for lifetimes and lifetimes. It wasn't just twenty years in the Mystery School; it was lifetimes of working, studying and suffering; lifetimes of loneliness and pain; lifetimes of being a servant to herself. She didn't want to get it wrong *now*, after all this time.

The path through the temple seemed endless as she continued walking slowly toward the figure. She could feel the Master's intense stare, eyes absolutely focused on her, watching every step. This made it even more frightening and intimidating. She wished so much that they had told her what to do or at least what to expect, but all they had said was, "When you hear the knock on the door, it's your time." So she continued, one hesitant step after the other.

Now, in her slow journey to the front of the temple, she found herself overcome by many, many thoughts. They were thoughts of her parents and the physical abuse she endured as a young girl; thoughts of her own anger and hatred of life and other people; thoughts of some of her darkest moments, even a time when she tried to take her own life. Why was all this coming back to her now, at this sacred and holy moment? She desperately tried to block these thoughts from her mind – "Not now, not now" – but they flooded over her. Perhaps she wasn't really as advanced as she thought. Perhaps she wasn't really ready for this moment. Perhaps she had made a mistake, but there was no turning back now. This was it.

She thought of the only true love she had ever really known; her dog. She had tried to find love with other humans, but it never seemed to work out. Her dog, however, was so loving, so much in service. Tears came to her eyes as she remembered him. "Why is it," she wondered, "That the one you love so much, that is so close, that you have opened your heart to, would die so young?" She was only eleven when her dog had passed away. "Why would God do such a thing?" she had often wondered.

On and on she continued, one slow step after the other, caught up more than ever in the barrage of thoughts that raced through her mind. She thought of when she left her husband and children, and of all the guilt and shame she had felt. What were they doing right now? What were they thinking? "How selfish I was for walking out on them," she thought. She began to remember past lives that were even more unpleasant than her current lifetime; so many lifetimes of searching, abuse and denial. "Why, oh why, are these thoughts coming over me now when I'm in the temple approaching the Master?" She wanted to scream, but instead she coughed. The sound reverberated off the walls and seemed to echo forever. She knew the Master was watching, and the student wondered if she had made some sort of mistake, if she had shown her weakness. But she continued to walk, feeling tired and weak, and wishing now that the knock on the door had never come. This was not a good day – or night – for her to meet the Master.

About five meters away from the Being standing in front of her, she stopped. What was she supposed to do now? She waited for some signal from the Master, some sign of what to do, but the Master's face was concealed in shadow. She couldn't even tell if it was a man or a woman. Feeling the intensity of the energy coming from the Master, she found herself wishing it would be a man. Then she thought, "How crazy that I'm having these thoughts. I bet the Master can hear them, and if the Master is a woman, now she's going to be upset with me."

She noticed the Master was wearing a hood and cape and, for a moment, she almost wanted to chuckle. "What a cliché – a temple, candles, the smell of old incense and here's the Master in a hood and cape."

Taking a few more steps now, her whole body tensed. Why, oh why, hadn't they told her what to do or at least given her some instructions? Why was this so difficult? Shouldn't this be a beautiful occasion filled with music and singing angels, flowers and lights everywhere? But no, it was just this cold, ancient empty temple with no one but the Master. She felt tears coming now, still not knowing what to do or if she was getting it right. She was closer to the Master now, and still so confused with all these chaotic thoughts streaming through her head. Why now? Why would these thoughts about old memories, pains and wounds be coming in now? Hadn't she done enough studying and healing to get rid of them? But here they were. "It must be a test," she thought, "To see if I'm worthy, to see if I can handle this intense energy."

She waited in silence; was she supposed to say something? How do you even address a Master? She wanted to scream out, "What do you want from me? What do you expect? What is this game?" She took a few more steps and now felt anger coursing through every part of her. Why had she ever joined this Mystery School in the first place? Why had she ever subjected herself to their stupid ways?

She took a few more steps and dared to look up for a moment, but in the darkness she still could not see the face of the Master. It still appeared to be just a hooded robe draped over a shadowy figure.

A few more steps and now she could actually smell the Master. It was a light, fragrant scent and, being this close to the Master, it was a very obvious contrast against her own heaviness. *The lightness of the Master was in such stark contrast to the darkness of herself.*

She stopped again, not knowing what to do. Should she reach out and touch the Master? Should she say something or wait for the Master to greet her? She felt confused and angry. *Why hadn't they told her what to do?* Finally, she broke down, sobbing in tears of defeat and ashamed that she couldn't control her emotions. Her cries echoed throughout the temple, bouncing off the walls, floor and ceiling as if she was sobbing in every corner of the massive room.

With tears streaming down her face, her body grew weaker and weaker until she finally fell to the ground. Curled up on the floor like an infant, the student wept like she hadn't done in ages. She was crying because she had failed whatever this test was they had given her; crying because she was overcome with the emotions of all the darkness in her life; crying because she just didn't know what to do anymore. Her body ached from the wracking sobs, her eyes burned from the tears flowing down to the floor.

"What is the Master thinking? Why don't they even offer to help me? Why doesn't someone come and scrape me off this cold, hard floor and drag me away from here?" It all felt so foolish, so stupid, and it seemed to go on forever and ever, this torment of dark thoughts and feelings of weakness, guilt and shame. She had failed right here in front of the Master, all these years and all her studies gone to waste. "Why me?" she thought bitterly. "Why on this night was I chosen? Why did I come so close, only to fail?"

Finally, after she had cried every last tear, after every last dark thought had come through her mind until there was nothing left, she took a breath. Slowly, she pulled herself up from the floor and decided, then and there, "No more. No more of this will I take, not from myself, not from some Master, not from some Mystery School. No more. I'm done. I'm finished feeling this way. *No more.*" And in that moment, she had not a single care in the world. She didn't even care about dying at this point, even though she knew what that felt like from trying to take her own life when she was younger. No, this was different. This had nothing left in it, no emotion, no desire, nothing. This was simply saying "No more." It was the final surrender. *No more!*

She stood up, brushed off her clothing, wiped her eyes so she could see once again, and now looked directly at the Master. Somehow, she could see more clearly than before, and barely discerned the outline of the face. Startled by what she saw, the student moved a little closer. At that very moment, the Master's head lifted and looked straight into her eyes – and suddenly everything fell into place. The student was looking into the eyes of her own Self. *She* was the Master!

It wasn't someone else. It wasn't a grand teacher or ascended being. It was her own Self all along. This was the night she had to face the fear of facing her Self, of being in the presence of her Free Self.

No wonder she had felt so small and weak. No wonder all those dark thoughts and feelings had come over her, because being in the presence of her Free Self had illuminated everything – all the trials and tribulations, all the pain, everything. All her searching and seeking, all the anticipation of one day meeting her Master, all the secrecy, anxiety and doubts, the whole wave of feeling unworthy, all the memories of the past flooding in; and all this time *she* had been the Master. It was always there. Nothing to achieve, nothing to attain. It was as simple as approaching her Free Self.

The Master had always been there, waiting. The Master never needed to give instructions or create any lessons; she was always there. The student took a deep breath and felt the connection, the familiarity with herself. She even had a bit of a smile on her face. There had been no test; everything was appropriate. That knock on the door wasn't from one of the teachers at the school or anyone else. It was from her Free Self, welcoming her back. It was time.

She stood there looking in amazement at the beauty of her own Self. She still couldn't make out the human facial details, but she could certainly feel the energy, love, acceptance and enlightenment of her Self.

Then she heard a sound, one that hadn't been there when she first entered the temple. It was a familiar, ancient, yet new sound. She took a deep breath and listened closely. It was two deep, resonant tones, sounding over and over again.

*Boom, boom.*

"What is it?" she thought. "Why does it seem so familiar? I know I've heard that sound before." It seemed to be coming from the Master, from her Free Self, but it also seemed to be coming from within her. "Maybe the sound was here when I first walked in, but I didn't hear it for being so nervous," she thought. "But now it's so clear and present. What is it?" As she listened closely, it felt more and more familiar. It had two notes, a beautiful simple rhythm, and it was constantly there, sounding again and again.

Then she remembered. "Ah, I know that tone! It's not my heartbeat; it's something beyond that. It is *'I Am.'* It is that constant reminder that was always, always there. *Boom, boom. I Am.* Nothing else matters. Not my past, not my future. I Am. I Exist, and I've always known this. They even talked about it in the Mystery School – the *I Exist* – but I never really heard it. It was just one of many phrases. But now I truly get it. *I Exist. Boom, boom.*

"I might be dead right now, for all I know. I might have died on the floor of this temple and left my physical body behind. I might have crossed over five minutes ago when I collapsed. Who knows? It doesn't even matter. But the fact is that *I Exist*. I am eternal. I Am that I Am.

"*I Exist!* Do you hear that, temple walls? Do you hear? *I Am that I Am! I Exist!* Do you hear that universe? Oh, universe, how I used to call out to you and it seemed you never heard me. Well, universe, I Exist! I don't care if you're there are not, *I Exist*.

*Boom, boom.*

"And memories, you stinking dark old memories, *I Exist*. You're just a memory. I Exist, and that's all that matters. I Exist, and I'll continue to exist. I'll continue to experience. I'll continue to have my knowingness. I Am that I Am. I am my Free Self and I always have been. I am my *own* Master; how silly that I ever looked to any others. I Am that I Am, flowing through and cleansing every part of me.

"Why did it take me so long to Realize? Why didn't I get that knock at the door a long, long time ago? Why was I in this Mystery School for twenty years?" Then she laughed with the answer, "Because I thought I had to be, because I chose it. I thought this was the way it had to be done."

*Boom, boom.*

Sitting there with herself – her Master Self – the student laughed, thinking about all the twists and turns she'd taken in her search, all the wild experiences and crazy thoughts, all the illusions of separation. She smiled, knowing that she had finally, finally come to enlightenment. It wasn't anything like she thought it was going to be. There were no rainbows and unicorns and cotton candy. It was just a big, old, stinky, incensed-filled temple. She thought it was going to be filled with ceremony and other people, but it was just her meeting her Self, finally realizing "I Am that I Am," finally just Allowing.

*Boom, boom.*

She laughed again, thinking about how difficult she had made it, and also how wonderful it was. Then she thought, "Would I change anything about it, now that I've allowed the Master to be here with me? Would I change anything about my journey?" Immediately, she knew the answer. "No. I just wish I had realized that the Master was always here. I wish I had allowed myself to know, no matter where my search took me, even to the point of taking my own life, that the Master was right here. Ah, what a game it has been, pretending that the Master was someone or somewhere else."

She laughed some more. "Why did I make it so difficult for myself? Why did I spend so much money on this crappy school? Why, oh why, did I feel so guilty about things? Those have got to be the worst human emotions – guilt and shame – but I guess I had some sort of fun with it. It really was my creation all along; there wasn't anything or anyone else imposing it on me."

*Boom, boom.*

Then she paused for a moment and exclaimed, "I hope I'm not dead!" She took a deep breath, felt the life within her body and realized, "No, I'm not dead; now I've got to go out and teach this! I have to go tell the other students I Exist! I've got to tell my family I Am that I Am! I've got to start a school of my own. I've got to write a book. I've got to teach classes. I ..." She caught herself and laughed, "Oh, shut up! Yes, I could do that, but they wouldn't hear it. I didn't hear it; why would they be any different? I could go teach some sort of healing, but do they really want to heal? I could go teach my own form of 'Ten Easy Steps to Mastery,' but I don't think they're really looking for ten easy steps. Ten difficult steps, perhaps. That's what they really want, but it doesn't make such a good brochure."

She took a deep breath and smiled, "Why didn't they just tell me?" Then she remembered they *had* told her, she just hadn't been able to hear it. She had found every reason and every excuse under the sun to avoid her own enlightenment. Oh, she had gotten angry with the teachers, because she thought they were withholding something important from her. She wanted them to them to provide the answers and the pathway and the keys to enlightenment. She remembered long debates with some of her teachers when she demanded, "Just give me the answer!" And they had, but she hadn't heard it.

Now she understood that "I Exist" *is* the enlightenment. It's not any more magical or esoteric or mystical or sacred than that. It's not delivered in a golden cup from heaven. It has always been here – *I Exist*. It really was that simple; she just hadn't allowed herself to realize it. I Exist *is* the enlightenment. Once you really realize that, once it's more than just a nice thought or a few words, once you can truly feel it – *I Exist* – that *is* the enlightenment. That's it; nothing else matters.

She took a deep breath and really let herself feel into that eternal tone – *I Am*. She let herself swim in it. She let it flow into her blood, into her thoughts, into her breath. She let herself remember that it had always been there. No matter how dark her experiences or how deep her guilt and shame had been, it was always there.

She took another deep breath, still standing there in the temple but now so fully integrated with her Self that there wasn't even a hooded figure anymore. It was all her. "Now what?" she mused. In the past, she would have always had some program to follow at this point – something to do, something to commit herself to, some promise to keep – but now she just smiled. She didn't need a program. She didn't need to write down ten steps or even one. It was all within her, in that ancient rhythm – *I Exist. I Am that I Am.*

*Boom, boom.*

She was free now, free of herself. You could say she was free of mass consciousness, but it was really of herself. She was free of this journey into embodiment, this birthing of herself. She had finally birthed the sovereign being. She was free.

What happened next didn't matter. She no longer had to find meaning to life. She didn't have to decide what to do next or figure out what would give her the greatest joy. She didn't have to think about any of that, because it didn't matter. It had no meaning. She didn't have to think about abundance, grace or happiness. "Such old terms," she thought. "Well, they are terms I used just thirty minutes ago, but they're really old now. The word 'happiness' doesn't even make sense when I'm a free being. There's no reason to define things in that way. *I Exist* is the only thing. What I do from now on doesn't matter. Whether I teach or just go swimming every day, whether I read books or sing – it doesn't matter. There doesn't have to be a meaning or a purpose."

She took a deep breath, blew out the candles in the temple, walked outside and closed the doors behind her. She lived many, many more years, not because she focused on staying young but because she was truly present in her body, in herself, and because she was free.

She traveled and lectured. She painted a lot. She often talked with the animals because she could finally communicate with nature. She did wonderful things, bizarre things, quiet things, anything. Life was never boring, because it was now filled with so many colors, dimensions and new, interesting relationships.

She was a Master, a true Ascended Master walking on Earth. She never mentioned that to anyone; it was her own private thing. She didn't want to make anything out of it and nobody would believe her anyway. They would have asked her to do something like walk on water or turn oil into dust or whatever other silly games humans play. She didn't need to tell anyone. She simply knew it. But others knew it too. Others who were in her presence knew there was something different about her. Some were afraid of her, because her presence was so clear, but some understood it. Some loved it. Some wanted to be close to her. Yes, some wanted to feed off of her too, and she was very clear with them: "You cannot." Some were drawn to her light like flies and started swarming around her. But, with the greatest compassion, she simply said, "Get away from me."

Then one day, she knew it was time. Not out of sadness or boredom, it was just time to leave the physical realm. She could have continued on living for many more years, but she knew it was time. She chose a date, although it had nothing to do with astrology or a birthday or anything else. She chose a date and on that day she simply vanished. She had tidied up everything and released her personal goods, and now there was nothing left behind, save for a pile of clothes on the floor.

And with her, she brought all the experiences of all of her lifetimes on Earth. The joy and the sadness, the love and the grief, the confusion, anxiety and lostness – she brought all these things with her. She embodied herself completely. And, to this very day, she's still present at times. She still comes by way of Earth, not in a physical body, but in her presence. To this day she still whispers to those who listen and says, "I Exist, and so do you, dear friend. I Exist, and so do you."

Take a moment now and breathe. Perhaps you can feel her presence with you, a true Ascended Master. She reminds you that you don't need to suffer or bring trauma into your life any more. There is no reason for anxiety and pain. She desires that you might also come to see yourself as the Master; that you might truly come to know and understand *I Exist*.

This is a story of a real human, now an Ascended Master.

Enjoy your experience into enlightenment. It will only happen once.

Take a good deep breath into the I Exist.

*Boom, boom.*

# Story 19

# The Park Bench

*Based on a friend's early morning experience...*

The Master sat on his favorite park bench waiting for the sun to come up over the hilltops. The sky was transforming from inky darkness to a fiery red that would eventually be replaced by the infinite blue sky. "This will be a busy morning," thought the Master, even though he would be spending it alone. It was the same bench where he had his profound Realization years ago, experiencing what some people call enlightenment. He preferred to simply call it Realization. Awareness of his awareness.

The Master's Realization had come to him like a breath – easy and graceful. He was expecting (and perhaps hoping for) a cosmic spectacle, complete with lightning bolts and angels, but it didn't happen that way. None of his studies could have prepared him for the moment of Realization, because none of his teachers were actually enlightened themselves. It had taken place on this very bench when, on a morning very similar to this one, he was Present and Allowing. Unlike his usual pattern, he wasn't thinking about yesterday or tomorrow and, for once, he wasn't trying to become enlightened. His was simply present in the moment. He wasn't trying to figure out life itself; he was in a state of total Allowing, open to his entire divinity.

Over the years, this park bench had become the timeless place where aspects of the Master's past and future lifetimes would come for counsel. Coming from other times and places, they would sit with him and share their tears, ask their endless questions, boil in frustration, expose their fears and anxieties, and try to convince the Master to share his magical elixir with them. Some of the aspects would come only for a brief moment, feeling uncomfortable in the light-shadow of the Master, while others would linger for hours. As the Master sat on the park bench this morning, he knew one thing was certain: they would come. They knew this spot, and they knew the Master came here often. It was like a spiritual counseling sofa for past and future lives of his and, no matter how lost they might be, they all knew how to get here. And the Master didn't mind, because it was all about him, anyway.

The Master sipped his hot café latte, warming his inners against the light chill of the early morning. The aspects would be waking up soon and making their way to him. Until then, he had a few quiet, peaceful moments to enjoy the rhythms of this early autumn morning. He smiled as he thought about the age-old question: Which comes first, the aspects or the Master? It was like the chicken and egg question, but much more personal. Does the Master come first and then create aspects of himself in order to experience life in a variety of ways? Or do the aspects come first and, through their life lessons and incarnations, make the Master? The Master's answer to the question depended on what day you asked him. Today's answer would probably be, "The Master came first, then created the aspects in order to explore the depths and richness of life." But every time he gave this answer, the aspects would rebel, insisting that it was they who brought him to Realization. "A never-ending debate," he thought, "And an interesting game of thrones."

The Master was also a teacher, and his favorite class to teach was called Aspectology; it was also one of the most challenging. He taught his students that the human Self has something called aspects. These are expressions or fragments of the Self that are designed to carry out certain tasks or live out various storylines. Every person has them. For instance, there is a functional and useful aspect that learns to drive a car. Another aspect knows how to operate a computer and use the Internet. Another has a job or career, and knows how to maneuver in the workplace environment. There are personality aspects for cooking and fitness and shopping and even sleeping/dreaming. There are masculine and feminine aspects within everyone, regardless of their physical gender. In fact, the list of aspects can be nearly endless. If you want to learn how to fly an airplane or ski the Alps, just create an aspect and watch how quickly they learn. It's the original form of artificial intelligence.

As you can see, these aspects are generally helpful, and they rarely create problems. However, humans also have a myriad of what the Master called gray or dark aspects, and it was these more troublesome aspects on which his teachings were focused. He knew all about them, because he had wrestled with plenty of his own and could speak from experience. Now, after his Realization on this very park bench years ago, he just had compassion for them, although this tremendous compassion didn't necessarily mean tolerance. No, the Master could be an intolerant son-of-a-gun at times, because he didn't allow others – not even his own aspects – to suffocate or steal his energy. They had their own energy, and his job was to help them find it.

While the usual, helpful aspects are what the Master called "integrated," meaning that they were generally compatible with the human Self, these other aspects could be very un-integrated. They came into being as a result of wounds – emotional, psychic or physical/emotional trauma at various times in one's life – and were now stuck energy. In their own way, these aspects were crying out for attention, like a little child screaming for its mother and creating a lot of chaos for everyone and everything around. These emotionally troubled and un-integrated aspects want to come home to the Self, but as long as they feel "home" isn't safe, they'll continue to act out. The Master often thought of these aspects as run-away children. They run away because of the chaos and dysfunction at home, and simply won't return until it's safe. In the most extreme cases, these aspects will loath and even hate the human Self.

However, since his Realization, the Master found that *all* the aspects came to him for counsel, to complain, or sometimes just to sit in the quiet space beside him. Some of the aspects just needed a break from their frantic human activities before they jumped back into the fray. Indeed, he remembered when he came here years ago as the Wanting-to-be-Spiritually-Wise-and-Powerful aspect. This aspect was so pitiful and lost, and the Master chuckled as he thought about all the makyo (spiritual distractions) this aspect carried, in spite of its underlying sincerity. The spiritual aspect was oh-so-righteous, yet afraid of its own shadow. It would tell the other human aspects that it was going to bring salvation to all of them through its spiritual pursuits; that it would heal them, make them wealthy, smart, powerful and whatever other promise it could think of. In fact, that spiritual aspect sounded very much like a politician – all hot air and little substance. The spiritual aspect also had grandiose notions of trying to save the world, which now caused the Master to roll his eyes at the very thought.

The sun was just peeking over the hilltops as the first aspect of the day approached the Master. The air around him got very still and cold, then felt like a vacuum trying to suck him in. The Master took a long drink of his café latte and breathed deeply, impervious to the tomblike energy lingering around him. "It's Dark," the Master thought to himself. Dark was the simple name he called this nefarious aspect, for Dark was just that: The darkest and most diabolical aspect of all. The Master heard many of his other aspects in words, but not so with Dark. He was beyond using the human language, preferring to communicate in thought energies, what some would call telepathic or psychic pulses. But if he had used words, Dark would have sounded something like this:

"Stupid old man! Here you are, still sitting on this same old park bench right where I left you last time. Are you still waiting for your enlightenment?" taunted Dark. "Hoping it will come before you die? Look at you, so old and feeble."

The Master took another deep breath of the crisp morning air. The breath brought every cell in his body into a symphony of light. He felt like his body was shimmering and glowing, almost in perfect resonance with the morning sun.

"I met your spiritual aspect," Dark continued. "He's adamant about his spiritual quest. It consumes him. He's afraid to let go of it, because then he would not exist. How many lifetimes has he been around, old fool? You and I both know that this flaccid spiritual aspect is just you, sitting here right now."

The Master realized that this was his second cup of coffee, because his bladder suddenly jumped into the conversation. "Time to go!" it warned. The Master let the warning pass. He had learned a long time ago that everything talked – from his body to his aspects to trees to other people's thoughts – but it wasn't his job to respond to every whim or whisper. Many sensitive people drive themselves mad by trying to attend to every voice they hear, but ultimately, the only voice the Master listened to was his I Am, his true inner voice. Unlike the noisy voices of everything else, the voice of the I Am made no sound at all. It was pure, silent knowingness.

"You know why I'm here," growled Dark. "It's the same reason I'm always here. You're weak, you're a relic, and soon you will die. This game of being a Master is coming to an end. It was a nice game, but without your gullible students you would be nothing."

The Master continued to watch the sun rising up over the hilltops. Listening to the ranting intrusion of Dark, he felt as though he was watching a movie from a distance on this otherwise quiet morning. He pulled a bagel from the paper bag on his lap and took a big bite, letting the movie play out.

"There are no tomorrows in death, human creature," mocked Dark. "When you die, you die. There is only darkness, only me."

The Master belched. The bagel was still warm and tasted especially good today. He'd have to remember to order the peanut butter and pumpkin bagel again. Who would have thought that peanut butter and pumpkin together would have such a sensual flavor?

Dark continued his assault. "You'll be exposed for this spiritual charade. The charlatan is always revealed. You pretend to teach people about enlightenment, but you're really doing it for the money. You had nothing before you started writing your lame books and teaching baseless classes, and now you have more money than any of your students. But all of it will go away when the mask comes off. Just wait; there will soon be a lawsuit against you and your insipid spiritual school."

The Master loosened the scarf around his neck as the sun began to warm his body. He had forgotten his hat this morning – he tended to be more forgetful than ever because so many things just weren't important anymore – and now he sighed with pleasure, feeling the warmth of the sun on his head.

"You're a fool, old man, but a smarter one than most. Somehow, you managed to get people to follow you without question. They're more foolish than you, so perhaps they're getting what they deserve. But you're smart enough to know why I'm here, and why I will be back until I get it. There's no use in pretending to ignore me, fool. You can feel everything I am conveying to you. You know what I want."

Two joggers, a young man and woman, nodded and waved to the Master as they passed by. The Master drew a breath through his nose and smelled their energy. The sense of smell was one of his favorites, especially since he'd discovered that he could smell energy, not just physical odors. The joggers' energy smelled so vibrant, like an English herb garden in May. The smell lingered in the Master's nose long after they jogged past.

"You don't deserve to have a soul," announced Dark. "You're weak in the flesh and feeble in the mind. You're afraid of power, because you know you're not strong enough to control it. You teach that power is an illusion, but, in fact, *you* are the illusion. You are my aspect, my subject, my slave. Give your soul unto me!"

"How long had Dark been around?" the Master wondered as he tossed a piece of his bagel to a friendly stray dog. Dark had been his greatest nemesis right up until his Realization, and now, Dark was one of his fondest memories. Oh, the voice of Dark had once pounded him day after day, year after year, lifetime after lifetime...

"You made all of this up, phony Master. None of it is real. You couldn't handle your miserable life, so you made up this thing called spiritual enlightenment. It's merely a closet within your mind where you've hidden yourself. I'm here to bring you back to your mind, your sense, back to the world from which you came. Your delusions will ruin your soul, so I am here to take it on the moment you fall asleep. Dare not sleep, old man, for I will come to you in your shabby dreams."

The Master yawned, even though he had slept well the night before. That was something he found a bit surprising about Realization. He yawned a lot, even though he rarely felt tired, but at some point he had come to understand the reasons for yawning: First, life didn't have the drama that it used to have, so the yawn was, perhaps, a slight expression of what he called "pleasant boredom." It was a bit of tranquility sprinkled with a dash of contentment. Second, it was a constant reminder of how easy life was now. *"Relax into Your Enlightenment"* declared the large sign over the main door of his school. After lifetimes of efforting and studying for his enlightenment, he had finally learned to simply relax into his enlightenment. It's a natural process, so why swim upstream, against the current? "Just relax into your enlightenment," he implored his students. But 93% of them still bought into the "No Pain, No Gain" philosophy. The Master sighed just thinking about all of the wasted energy and needless suffering.

Dark's bravado started to wobble now. He sounded like a bad mobile phone connection, breaking up and distorted by a scratchy electronic noise. The Master knew that Dark was fading back into the putrid abyss from whence he came. Soon, some other aspects would come around, but none were so intimate and endearing as Dark. He tried so hard! He blew so much hot air! He smelled so foul and had a way of sucking the energy right out of the air. Dear, dear Dark! What a gift he had been to the Master.

A gaggle of lovely white geese made their way towards the Master, pecking at the ground for morsels of grass and crumbs of bagel. The Master stood up and stretched his arms and legs. He had been sitting for over an hour, although it felt like only a few minutes. Funny how time was so fluid now, he thought. There was a time when the Master rode the narrow and rigid tracks of Time, but now it was just another flexible thread of his reality construct.

Standing next to the park bench, taking a break between today's aspects, the Master allowed himself to feel deeply into Dark. There was a time when, as an awakening human, the Master was terrified of Dark. He cowered in the light out of fear that Dark would consume him and certainly commandeer his soul. As a matter of fact, one of his final hurdles into Realization was something called "Allowing." In Allowing, the Initiate lets go of everything and simply *allows* the Free Self – the I Am, what some people call their divinity – into their life.

At first, it sounded surprisingly simple, but it proved to be much more challenging than the Master could have imagined. The act of Allowing causes the Initiate to confront his or her deepest fears. The fears were always there, but the Initiate blocks them. Allowing brings them to the forefront, and then the Initiate has the choice of Allowing – which might open the door to an overwhelming Darkness – or Filtering. In the midst of this dilemma, the Initiate eventually realizes that there can be no compromise. It was *all* Allowing or *no* Allowing. There will be Realization, or there will be darkness.

The Master had chosen Allowing. It was a choice that came from his deep innate knowingness that there was more – *so* much more – to life and Self and creation. This is when he finally met Dark face to face, breath to breath, and encountered the biggest surprise of his life. *He was shocked to realize that Dark was his divinity.* Dark was actually the most sacred and compassionate part of himself that he had ever known, for it was within the darkness that he and all of his human lifetimes had dumped everything they hated about themselves. Every fragment of guilt and shame were tossed into this landfill of the soul. Every feeling of worthlessness, every loathing of self, every unforgiven thought or deed had been relinquished to Dark; abandoned in this rotting pit by the human who couldn't bear to love that part of themselves. But Dark held it, carried it and accepted it on behalf of the human, out of love for the human. Dark took the insults and abuses from the religious aspects who, in their fear, tossed Dark into the fires of hell. Dark loved and accepted everything the human despised about themselves.

"The darkness is your divinity. It is all that has gone unloved, held in the compassionate arms of your divinity, until you were ready. Now you are ready." The Initiate heard these words in his moment of Allowing. He broke down crying, for what seemed like days, as he came to realize the true meaning of compassion. Dark was not an evil force trying to seduce him; it was everything he had not loved about himself.

When the crying faded away, the Initiate realized he was now the Master. Never again would he fear the darkness. Never again would he fear himself. Without the fanfare of trumpets or the theatrics of lightning bolts, the Initiate was now a realized Master. Dark had proven to be the greatest gift he could have imagined.

The Dark aspect still came around sometimes, like he had done today, but it never phased or bothered the Master. As a matter of fact, he looked forward to it, because he knew some good was being done somewhere. Every time Dark came around, it was merely an aspect belonging to a past life or future life, but not his.

The Master untied his shoestrings in order to get more comfortable before his next session with an aspect. He sat back down on the park bench. "I am always here for you," he radiated, sending a telepathic message across time and space to all of his incarnations. "I am always here for me."

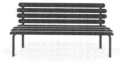

# Story 20

# End of the Day

*Inspired by the Master within...*

The Master retired to his room after a long day of teaching, counseling, answering endless questions and wiping a few tears from the eyes of his students. He had taken an hour to himself for fishing, one of his favorite pastimes, but the day was mostly occupied with guiding his students.

He poured a glass of fine French wine and slumped into his big lounge chair. Now, it was finally his own time. He kicked off his sandals, clicked the remote control to play soothing music, took a few deep breaths and let out a very big sigh. It's not always easy being a Master, he thought to himself with a chuckle. But he wouldn't trade it for anything in the world, or in the universe for that matter.

The Master slowly slipped into a familiar and comfortable zone, somewhere between this world and the other realms. This was his place, his private dimension. This was where he replenished his energy, something that was very important to do after working with humans all day. Humans feed off of other people's energy, he thought. Someday they will learn that they don't need to do that. Someday they will be free.

A smile came across his face as he pondered his work. "Why do I do it?" he asked himself. "Why work day after day with students on the spiritual path, some of whom are filled with so much makyo that, at times, it seems they are light years away from enlightenment? Why deal with students who claim they are seeking the truth when, indeed, they are only seeking power?"

It certainly wasn't for the money, because abundance came to him effortlessly and without the need to charge his students. It wasn't for the feeling of accomplishment, because many of his students would not even become Realized in this lifetime. And it wasn't because he actually liked teaching this thing called spirituality. It was tedious and repetitive at times and, at other times, maddening with its emotions and drama. Plus, he had always known this work wasn't about spirituality. The students liked to think they were becoming spiritual, but, eventually, they would learn that there was no word in the human language that could define what he loosely called "Realization." No word had ever been created for coming to the timeless sovereignty of your soul. How he loathed human words at times. The ability to define concepts is a reflection of consciousness, and the human language had so very few words that would even begin to define what he taught.

Back to the question, he mused. Why *did* he do this work??

The answer was easy. There had been a time when he was the student, when he was stuck – maybe imprisoned was a better word – in his five physical senses and his mind. There had been a time when he wasn't free, or at least he had believed himself to not be. There had been a time when he was in so much physical and emotional pain, a pain caused by knowing there was more, but not knowing what it was, that he could barely make it through a human day. He remembered the desperation and fragility of those times. He thought about how he struggled, using all of his will in the effort to overcome the human condition. He had prayed and meditated; he had become a vegan, a fruitarian and, for a very short period, a breatharian until he collapsed from hunger, all in a futile attempt to find the answers.

He finally came to realize that the human cannot ever find the answers, because the human isn't responsible for their enlightenment. It was a shocking revelation for him. *The human isn't responsible for their enlightenment.* Enlightenment comes from the passion of the soul. "Crap," he thought to himself. "There I go using those old words like soul. There is no soul, at least not in terms of how people think of it. There is the 'I Exist.' Nothing else matters."

He took another sip of wine and sank deeper into his chair. Soon, it would be midnight and another day would begin. For most people, it would be just like the previous day. The calendar would say it's a new day, but their lives would be pretty much the same as every other day. But then one day, something would happen to change them for all eternity. It's called awakening, and nothing would ever be the same again. These are the people he worked with, the ones who came into awakening, whether by choice or by chance. It would be the most challenging time of any lifetime they had ever lived, but also the most beautiful experience they would ever have. It almost seemed unfair that awakening felt so brutal when, indeed, it was so beautiful.

He worked with those who had come to their awakening. He helped guide them on their journey to mastery and, eventually, into their Magi-ship. The ones that make it, that is. Many would never get out of the awakening phase in this lifetime. Some would spend four, five or even more lifetimes in the awakening phase before they moved into their mastery. Awakening is such a dragon, he thought! If only his students realized that the dragon guarding the doorway to enlightenment was simply a metaphor for clarity. But the dragon had a nasty habit of scaring the hell out of students who made it to the doorway. He chuckled to himself, because his dragon was now his favorite pet, sleeping quietly beside the fireplace in his room. How funny, he thought. The fire-breathing dragon that once tormented him day and night now slept peacefully beside the fireplace.

Millions of pages have been written by metaphysical authors and teachers about the spiritual journey, but mostly by people who are not enlightened. Their words were an attempt to define what they had not yet experienced or realized. In other words, a lot of well-meaning makyo. The Master had learned that it came down to just two simple words. Yes, the totality of enlightenment in two simple words: *Allow* and *and.*

**Allow**: The human cannot possibly imagine enlightenment. It is beyond the realm of the mind, and that's a good thing, because the mind would attempt to take it hostage, control and limit it. But the human can *allow* it. They can allow the magic of the I Am into their 3D mortal lives. They can stop planning, studying, efforting and manipulating their way into enlightenment, and simply allow their divinity (for lack of a better word) to be with them. The human turned their back on divinity a long time ago and, in honor of that choice, their divinity then turned its back on them. *That* is true compassion! Now, the student can simply allow their divinity back into their everyday human life, no matter how little money they have; no matter how many warts and hang-ups they see in the mirror; no matter how holy or un-holy they are; no matter if they have bad breath or bad posture. The only responsibility of the human is to allow everything about themselves, and then get out of the way.

**And**: The human perceives themselves as singular. They think they are a human on the path to some spiritual destination and, therefore, they are. But once the human allows themselves to realize they are many rather than one; that they are the student *and* the Master, it frees them from the singularity and restrictions they have come to accept. It means you are never trapped in limitation again and, up till now, the entire human journey has been about limitation.

**And**: You are male *and* female. You are the light *and* the dark. You are a genius *and* a fool. You are in the present moment *and* in the past *and* in the future. You are in the midst of many experiences at the same time, never again singular; never again solely linear. Within you, you are already enlightened *and* you are the student just setting out on the path.

Singularity, and its cousin linearity, are so painfully limiting. Humans have come to believe that they are moving from Point A to Point B, but, in reality, they are at Point A *and* Point B *and* moving from point A to B. *And* is the key to the prison cell. It frees you to be all things, not just one. *And* isn't a concept or a spiritual cliché; it's actually the way of creation. Wasn't it somebody like God who said, "I Am the Alpha *and* the Omega"? Even God understood the concept of *and* – "I am here *and* I am there."

"It's so simple," thought the Master, "*And* it's so difficult. *And. Multiple. Free.* I Am ALL That I Am."

The Master dozed off in his big comfortable chair *and* in his other realm. So simple enlightenment is. So funny how people deliberately attempt to make it so hard. Maybe they think they've earned it if they work hard at it.

It's all about Allowing and *and*. Why write millions of words when it comes down to two? As the Master slipped into the deeper realms of his nocturnal travels, he thought to himself, "Maybe I'll just write a short little book filled with stories about true experiences with my students. It's certainly better than writing a million words and, besides, a book with just two words won't sell very well. Perhaps I'll call it *Memoirs of a Master*? Or maybe I'll just dream about writing it. That's a lot less work."

Good night, dear reader. Oh-Be-Ahn (the greeting from one multi-dimension traveler to another as they pass through the corridors of Time, Space and Beyond).

Oh-Be-Ahn.

# Other Books
# by Geoffrey Hoppe
with Adamus Saint-Germain and Tobias

**Act of Consciousness** – *Adamus Saint-Germain*
Life is an act. We act like humans, and therefore experience like humans with a litany of limitations, shortcomings and drama that mask our underlying angelic consciousness. It's an unnatural act, but we accept it as reality. However, acting like a Master will literally change the type of energy we attract into our lives, and therefore change the reality in which we exist and experience.

**Live Your Divinity** – *Adamus Saint-Germain*
A new dimension in spiritual teaching, this intriguing and provocative book will challenge your perceptions of reality, remind you of forgotten truths, and prod you toward the realization and manifestation of your divine nature here on Earth.

**Masters in the New Energy** – *Adamus Saint-Germain*
This profound and delightful book is filled with insightful and practical information about living as true Masters in the New Energy. Adamus' simple and profound messages provide the guideposts for those who choose to go beyond limited thoughts and beliefs into a new understanding of reality.

**Journey of the Angels** – *Tobias*
Learn how and why we became separated from Spirit, what transpires in the angelic realms, and discover a new and refreshing picture of why Earth was created and why we chose to come here. This profound material will reawaken memories that have been buried since the beginning and help you remember the answers to the most basic

questions about life. *Journey of the Angels* speaks to the deepest parts of you and will awaken you to the divine purpose that brought you into this lifetime.

**Creator Series – *Tobias***
*"You never go Home. Instead, Home comes to you."* With these words Tobias laid out an entirely new understanding of how we came to Earth and why this is such an important crossroads on our spiritual journey. The Creator Series is full of practical tools for thriving as an awakening being on Earth.

# Other Courses

with Adamus Saint-Germain

### DreamWalker™ Death Transitions

This three-day school, offered by certified teachers, teaches how to guide friends, family and clients through the death process into the non-physical realms, providing comfort and love to make their transition more peaceful. This School offers certification as a DreamWalker Death Guide.

### DreamWalker™ Birth Transitions

This three-day school is offered by certified teachers as well as through a Personal Study Course. Saint-Germain defines the birth process from conception to post-birth with a focus on the spiritual selection aspects. This School offers certification as a DreamWalker "Adoula" Guide.

### DreamWalker™ Ascension Transitions

Adamus Saint-Germain's three day Ascension School provides unique and personal insights into the nature of Ascension and the implications of the last lifetime on Earth. This course is offered by certified DreamWalker Ascension teachers.

### DreamWalker™ Life

Adamus Saint-Germain's three day DreamWalker Life School provides insights on how to truly live in and love life. Through Quantum Allowing and the grace of the crystal flame of transfiguration, attendees learn what it means to be a Master on Earth. This course is offered by certified DreamWalker DreamWalker Life teachers.

### New Energy Synchrotize™

Adamus Saint-Germain says Synchrotize goes "beyond hypnosis" for those who want to consciously create their reality. Synchrotize is offered as a Personal Study Course. The study process takes four consecutive days to complete.

### Standard Technology

Adamus Saint-Germain and Tobias join together to present Standard Technology, a New Energy program for activating your body's natural rejuvenation system. Standard Technology is offered as a Personal Study Course.

### The Master's Life (Series)

In this ongoing series of presentations, Adamus Saint-Germain discusses the embodied enlightened life and provides support and inspiration in dealing the challenges of staying here on planet Earth.

# Additional Courses and Material
available through the Crimson Circle

## Tobias' Sexual Energies School

This three-day school focuses on what Tobias calls the "sexual energy virus." It helps the student understand how people energetically feed off of each other, and how to release the chain of the virus. This is one of the most basic and important courses offered by the Crimson Circle. It is taught by certified teachers worldwide.

## Tobias' Aspectology School

In this three-day workshop, Tobias focuses on the Aspects or parts of self that negatively affect and sometimes control our lives due to trauma, whether in this or a past life. Learn tools to help you integrate these energies and bring true freedom to your life. This core material is taught by certified Crimson Circle teachers worldwide.

## Tobias' Journey of the Angels School

In this profound school, given three weeks before his departure, Tobias weaves together the core of all his teachings over the previous 10 years. Offering a completely different perspective on everything you learned in church and school, this school will change your concept of what being human really is.

**Single and Multi-Session Audio Products** Tobias, Kuthumi and Adamus cover a broad range of topics in dozens of recorded presentation. Varying in length from an hour or less to 15 or more hours of channeling, these life-changing sessions are also available with translations in nearly 20 languages.

**Monthly Shouds** Text transcripts or audio recordings of all channeled monthly messages since August 1999 are available *free of charge* on the Crimson Circle web site (www.crimsoncircle.com). The Shouds are channeled in annual series (The Creator Series, The New Earth Series, The Divine Human Series, etc.) and also include many Question and Answer sessions. The Shouds are an excellent record of Shaumbra's journey since the beginning of the Crimson Circle.

**Workshops** Geoffrey and Linda Hoppe present workshops around the world featuring live channelings with Adamus Saint-Germain, Kuthumi and Merlin. Check the Crimson Circle web site for dates and details: www.crimsoncircle.com/Calendar.

# About Adamus Saint-Germain

Saint-Germain (also sometimes referred to as Master Rakoczi) is a spiritual Master of the Ancient Wisdom credited with mystical powers and longevity. He is also identified with the real life person known as the Count of St. Germain (1710–1784) who lived throughout Europe in the 18th century and was active in many of the Mystery Schools of the time. He adopted his name as a French version of the Latin "Sanctus Germanus," meaning "Holy Brother." Saint-Germain teaches that the highest alchemy is the transformation of one's human consciousness into the divinity of the Higher Self.

Over the years, much has been written and many stories told of this intriguing, somewhat enigmatic figure in history. He is a remarkable being who has manifested in many lifetimes and identities on Earth. In his lifetime as St. Germain, he was born in an area now known as Spain to a Jewish Portuguese father and a mother of royal Spanish lineage. He traveled throughout Europe counseling kings and other royalty, and was known as a great alchemist – a great mover of energy.

In 2005 Saint-Germain came to the Crimson Circle organization as a guest of Tobias, another Ascended Master, channeled by Geoffrey Hoppe. After Tobias' reincarnation to the physical realms in July 2009, Saint-Germain took over his teaching and guidance role with the Crimson Circle. In his work with the Crimson Circle, he refers to himself as Adamus Saint-Germain in order to differentiate his contemporary teachings related to embodied ascension from his previous work and previous channelers. Adamus is a unique facet of Saint-Germain's oversoul. His style is provocative, entertaining and deeply insightful. His passion is to assist those who have clearly chosen embodied enlightenment in this lifetime, yet are faced with the myriad distractions and doubts that stem from today's intense mental focus and programming coupled with the density of mass consciousness.

# About Geoffrey & Linda Hoppe

**Geoffrey Hoppe**: The early spiritual curiosity of a young man was all but forgotten as he served a few years in the US Army as a Public Information Specialist at the NASA Ames Research Center (Mountain View, California), and then stepped into the business world. After finding his way to senior management positions in several advertising agencies, Geoffrey started his own marketing company in Dallas, Texas at the ripe old age of 28. Later on, he co-founded an aviation telecommunications company (provider of Internet services for business jets and commercial airlines, now known as Gogo), serving as Vice President of Sales and Marketing until 2001. In a stroke of ironic prescience, Geoffrey holds three patents for multidimensional telecommunications technologies, as well as numerous trademarks and copyrights.

**Linda Hoppe**: A gifted artist and highly creative by nature, Linda graduated Summa Cum Laude and went on to teach Art Education, even writing a ground-breaking curriculum for Texas' first high school honors Art Education program. Her artistic talents landed her a job as Fashion Merchandise Manager with a Fortune 500 company, helping to set the styles and designs for each upcoming season. She also served as manager for Geoffrey's marketing consulting company for several years.

**Destiny**: Geoffrey & Linda met in high school and got married in 1977 on the day the first Star Wars movie premiered. Twenty years later, an angel named Tobias introduced himself to Geoffrey during an airplane flight. After talking and learning together for an entire year, Geoffrey finally told Linda about his invisible friend. Soon after, Tobias started working with clients of a local psychologist, providing deep insights into past lives and current challenges.

In late summer 1999, a few friends were invited to listen as Tobias spoke through Geoffrey, assisted by Linda. It was the beginning of the Crimson Circle, an organization that they would soon spend every waking moment trying to keep up with. Since then, Crimson Circle has grown into a multinational organization, with Geoffrey & Linda traveling the globe conducting numerous workshops and events each year.

They didn't see it coming, but looking back in hindsight, they wouldn't change a thing in this most extraordinary lifetime.

# The Crimson Circle

I've often been asked, "What is the Crimson Circle?" Words escape me. My tongue gets twisted and my brain starts to spin. How can I describe something so deep – yet simple – and something so outside the realm of normal human thinking? How can I share the thousands of stories about humans around the world coming into their embodied enlightenment, and what the heck is embodied enlightenment anyway?

I used to launch into a long explanation, oftentimes losing my listener when I tried to explain the quest for truth, the wisdom of the Ascended Masters, our *real* purpose for being here on Earth at this time, the dynamics of channeling, the difference between consciousness and energy... well, you get the point. I got way too mental.

Now I just say, "You know what it's like... when you know there's more to life, but you just don't know what it is? That's what the Crimson Circle is about." Somehow people just get it. It saves me a lot of anguish and it saves them a lot of tedious explanation.

And, there is something more to life, no matter what your five senses and mind tell you. There is a Beyond and you're not crazy for thinking that there is. You were just trying to find it with your current senses. Once you allow yourself to go beyond your current senses, you'll come to realize that *there is so much more*.

Learn more about the Crimson Circle at www.crimsoncircle.com

–   *Geoffrey Hoppe, channeler for Adamus Saint-Germain*

*"All is well in all of Creation –*
*because* ***you*** *are here."*
- Adamus Saint-Germain

# Notes

# Notes

55833610R00095

Made in the USA
Middletown, DE
12 December 2017